To: Dan. I hope *enjoying*
a few laughs, *♡* W9-AVQ-655

Herb Hyde (signature)

HERBIE

HERBIE

A TROY YOUTH'S COMING OF AGE

SORT OF!

Herbert Hyde

Edited by Jeanine McCartan
Cover art by Herbert Hyde
Author photo by Robert Scully
Photos of Saint Paul's Episcopal Church by Paula Hebert
Cover and book design by The Troy Book Makers

To order additional copies of this title, contact your favorite local bookstore or visit www.tbmbooks.com

ISBN: 978-1-61468-264-6

Acknowlegements

I would like to thank Jeanine Mccartan for her tireless work editing my manuscript. Without her help this book would not have been published. I also want to than my wife Barbara who graciously allows me to follow my passion in life. I would also like to thank my buddies who helped bring these stories to life. Thanks: Alan, Billy, Charlie, Carl and Denny.

Reflection and Dedication

Procrastination is the bane of all who wish not to. Here I am doing exactly what I said I wouldn't do. It's not writer's block. It's just that I'm a block head writer. I promised myself I would go forward. But then I got stuck in a rut along the way, and that rut was the tree of life which I had to navigate. My father was a lumber jack by trade and he worked felling trees so we might have food in our bellies and clothes on our backs. However, it didn't *always* work out that way because a gin mill might occasionally jump in front of him on his way home from work. The good thing back then was there were a lot of trees in the world. Otherwise, I wouldn't be writing this story. I would have starved to death!

Can you remember the first time you smelled something and then tried to duplicate that sensation? Those first sensations become an imprint on the beautiful canvas of our lives. I remember writing in my first book that each day was a new sensory adventure for me as a toddler. "I might wake up to the sound of Ma bustling about the kitchen getting breakfast ready, the smell of hickory-smoked bacon cooking in her cast iron skillet, and the aromatic fragrance of that 'Good to the last drop' Maxwell House coffee percolating on the stove. If I slept late, I might awaken to the sweet smell of Ma's apple or mince meat pies wafting through my room."

Sixty years later I slowly walked down Congress Street, my arthritic back, aching and arched forward, making me appear several inches shorter than I am. I was out trying to peddle my first book, College and Eighth to any store owner who would be willing to take it on consignment such as Famous Lunch, Manory's, Beat Shop, Clemente's Frame Shop and Java Hut up by School 14.

Walking past a tattered storefront with its faded green paint, peeling and rendering itself to dust at mother-nature's behest, I was struck by a sweet smell from the past that touched my soul. A sensation I often hoped to replicate but could never accomplish, no matter how hard I tried. I squinted through the darkened windows of this dilapidated diner and could almost see balding, gray-haired men and matronly-looking women in printed dresses, laughing heartily at well-worn jokes and stories. The muted sound of Christmas carols drifted all around. My mind drifted back to my early life when I first experienced that emotional, sensory arousal to something I never experienced before and believed I would never experience again.

The sweet, pungent aroma and that feeling of enlightenment had not been lost to the ages. Instead, it had sequestered itself in a distant corner of my life's palette, awaiting its chance to flutter back into my life like a wispy, colorful butterfly and repeat the instant joy I felt that first time. You see, today God in all his graciousness had given me a sense of newness and renewal in my aching and aging body, a body bearing the scars and burdens of a difficult but rewarding life. All the trials and tribulations I had faced during my life softly faded into the distant past, as I was drawn back to the innocence of my earliest memories. No more sadness, no more pain from the recent loss of my loving sister and surrogate Mom, Dorothy and my closest sister, dance partner, and dear friend Brenda. My heart was aching knowing my family was dwindling and I was now the oldest sibling left. How would I handle the responsibility of now being the family patriarch?

Retrieving that lost sensation and the instant joy I felt at this wondrous moment lifted dark clouds of pain and swept in a glorious burst of sunlight and beauty. Although it would not last forever, I was able to retrieve that missing ingredient that signifies the goodness and happiness of what life should be. Now I can complete my life's journey, knowing that what lies ahead will not be a burden because life's past becomes prologue. Now I can continue to write my life's story.

I am dedicating this book to my sisters Kathleen Zayachek, Dorothy Iacketta and Brenda Robinson.

Contents

Reflection and Dedication...v

One • Romancing the Stone Wall...1

Two • We are the Freshmen..5

Three • When Harry Met Charlie 9

Four • Booze, Drugs, Blackjack and Jail 13

Five • The Lovely Maidens...17

Six • A Change, of Course 29

Seven • Ivan Who and Study Hall Drama 33

Eight • What's the Deal with Football?..37

Nine • A Strapping Jock 41

Ten • Friday Night Duh-lights!..47

Eleven • Eggs Are No Yoke..51

Twelve • Catch a Fleeting Star...53

Thirteen • Sonny's Wedding and My First Official Kiss..................61

Fourteen • Pudding Ego Before Brains..67

Fifteen • Broadway Abe 69

Sixteen • High School/PTU /Service/Jail 73

Seventeen • Tiny Tim 77

Eighteen • I Get the 'Kurse' 81

Nineteen • Bucksters..87

Twenty • Wine, Wine, Water, Water—Dispensation for Life 89

Twenty-One • VD and Me? 95

Twenty-Two • Tuck Mashington...................................... 109

Twenty-Three • Bigots! Who Knew? 115

Twenty-Four • Laura Bunson 123

Twenty-Five • Popping, Fresh Dickie Tomain.................. 131

Twenty-Six • Hi Tech: the Scanner, the Times are Changing......... 137

Twenty-Seven • My Worst Sunburn in History................ 145

Twenty-Eight • Cruising!.. 155

Twenty-Nine • At the Car Wash..................................... 161

Thirty • For Christmas Sake 165

Thirty-One • Well, Hello...Dotty! 171

Thirty-Two • There Once Was an Indian Maid 175

Thirty-Three • Margie the Drill Sargent 179

Thirty-Four • Colonial/Hockey/Frat Parties 181

Thirty-Five • The Return of Yummy!.............................. 185

Thirty-Six • Cents of Worth 189

Thirty-Seven • Why Did He Go?.................................... 193

Thirty-Eight • Boy, Did I Get Fried!.............................. 199

Thirty-Nine • Broadening my Interests? 201

Forty • Oh, Henry!... 209

Forty-One • For the Good Times.................................... 211

Forty-Two • And Now the End Draws Near 213

Forty-Three • And So It Ends... 217

Forty-Four • One Door Closes and Another Opens.......... 221

Afterword.. 223

CHAPTER ONE

Romancing the Stone Wall

The weeks leading up to the start of high school were filled with both angst and excitement. The last day of Troy's summer basketball league was held on a hot, humid August afternoon. I was sitting on the long, white, concrete and stone wall guarding the entrance to Prospect Park with Tony Yates. We had just finished playing a team from South Troy in a game of shirts and skins. The skins won, and I had the sunburn to prove it.

Tony was my longtime friend and soon to be high school classmate. We reminisced about all the fun we had during our youth as we chugged ice cold bottles of coke Tony had commandeered from his uncle's store, located directly across the street from us. We kidded each other about how we use to fantasize about feeling up girls in the pool each summer like the older guys bragged about. However, neither of us ever got up the courage to even try it. We were too wimpy. Instead we'd watch the older guys, who always bragged about doing it, get slapped in the face when they tried. The thought of getting unceremoniously slapped in the face was a major deterrent for us.

The long white wall we were sitting on was an iconic place. Not just to Tony and me, but to hundreds of Ida Hill kids who had used it as their hangout over the years. A special meeting place we all would remember well into adulthood. Tony had attended St Francis De Salle's grade school, located right across the street from the wall, with Karen Finnigan and Sandy Stroh. I went to School 14, which was only a few short blocks away, with Jeannie Callahan, Billy Finch and all my other neighborhood buddies. I would soon lose some of my School 14 classmates and neighborhood buddies. Denny Barrow would attend La Salle, or as we used to call it, "Little Sissy's Institute." Others would go to Catholic High, located in Lansingburg.

I came to find out both Karen and Sandy were tough tomboys, reminiscent of my sister Patty. They too would kick the snot out of kids who would try to pull stuff with them. I remember when Karen whacked Billy Finch one wintery Friday night in the old wooden shack at Beldon's Pond. I think he was trying to get away with telling a dirty joke that went a bit over the line.

"Jesus, Karen! Why the hell did you do that? That hurt. " Billy whined, rubbing his now red and slightly swollen cheek.

"I did it because you're a jerk, Billy! Don't try to pull the same crap with me that you get away with those dirt bags you hang around with down by the train tracks. It won't work. Get it?" She then smacked him again, this time on the arm to reinforce what she was saying. Billy just grimaced and slinked away to the farthest corner of the shed to lick his wounded pride. Charlie Coots and Alan Sydner stood by laughing hysterically and called him a wimp.

Ice skating at Beldon's Pond was the thing to do for Ida Hill kids on a wintery Friday night. It was located just off Pawling Avenue and you had to climb down about seventy, ice- covered wooden stairs to reach it. Inside the shack was a big pot-belly stove used to warm your hands and feet after skating on the ragged, icy pond. The kids would voluntarily shovel any snow that might have accumulated during the week. Once that chore was completed they would form a line and begin skating in circles. The line might have been small in the beginning but as more kids joined in the line would become very long. Now if you were at the end of the line you had to skate like hell to keep up. If you couldn't, you would end up careening into a huge pile of snow that circled the rink.

Occasionally some of the guys would play hockey at the end of the rink. Other kids might go roaming near the Poestenkill Creek.

That was a very dangerous thing to do because you never knew when the ice would become too thin and you might end up in the drink. I'm sure over the years many kids had to be fished out of its murky depths before they died of hypothermia. Some of the guys who didn't want to bother going into the shed to use the bathroom would artistically spray paint the snow in intricate, golden patterns only they could appreciate. This was usually done in secluded areas near the infamous, haunted Mt. Ida Cemetery.

By ten o'clock most kids would finish their skating then head off for home or one of the local, Ida Hill haunts to hang out. Lily's ice cream parlor was a great spot for hot fudge sundaes or a black cow after a hard night's skating. Others might stop by Pojoe's store on the corner of Congress and Christy to snag a candy bar, bullshit, and inevitably get thrown out because they managed to tick off the owner for being too rowdy.

Some of the older guys like Billy, Charlie and Allen inevitably managed to con their way into Walsh's Grill for beer and a game of darts. No one seemed to care if you were a bit under age at the time, as long as you had the money to pay for it. Besides, usually one of their neighbors would be sitting at the bar getting their usual snout full of booze for the weekend. If you gave them the money, they would happily buy a round of drinks, as long as you paid for theirs.

Tony soon left, but I didn't want to head home just yet. Instead, I lay back on the tinder dry mound of tree roots interspersed among golden shafts of rye and crabgrass that had been a brilliant emerald green in the spring. With my hands tightly interlocked behind my head, I lazily glanced through the overhanging branches of the century-old maple and oak trees that lined the edge of the park. I tried to figure out what each wispy cloud formation resembled as it slowly drifted by. My eyes began to grow heavy. Before I knew it, I had drifted off into a fitful sleep where pictures of the past moved by as nimbly as the clouds passing by in the summer sky.

With tears silently drying in the corners of my tightly clenched eyes, I thought my nightmare was over. However, I was brought back to the present by a horrendous explosion. Within seconds a brilliant splash of molten, liquid gold erupted behind my tender eyelids. The atmospheric convergence of heat and light now seared my heart with fear. I awoke to a summer storm that within a few short moments would turn into a deluge of epic proportions and hurl a tsunami of mud and debris down Congress Street. I quickly gathered my wits and raced across to Pojoe's store to wait out the storm.

Those dreams and the ensuing storm that followed signified a turning point for me. I had to put my early childhood memories aside and forge a new way forward as a teenager. I could not turn back. It wouldn't be easy but I had to march on and begin the next leg of my life's journey: high school!

CHAPTER TWO

We are the Freshmen

Soon classes started and I became ensconced in my new and exciting life as a teenager. First the freshman dances where I still found myself sitting on the sideline with my friends. Seems like we all lacked the self-confidence to ask girls to dance at first. During that first dance, Larry and Billy kept badgering me to ask a cute little brunette named Sharon Manderville to dance. Sick of listening to their incessant yapping, I gave in and asked her to dance, but she smiled and politely turned me down. Of course, my ego was instantly shattered. From that point on I rarely asked girls to dance or out on dates. Besides, if I asked them out on dates, where would I get the money to take them? In the back of my mind I feared rejection. This would be a pattern that haunted me during high school. Ironically, that same girl who rejected me eventually became Larry's girlfriend and wife later in life. Go figure.

Oh by the way. I didn't stop going to dances with the guys. I was just not very successful finding girls who seemed interested in me. Maybe I was just too boring. Or maybe I wasn't good looking enough, with my new-fangled, horned-rimmed glasses. Thank God, I managed to permanently break them that summer. The second dance we decided to go to that year turned out to be a real eye opener. Ironically, that week's dance coincided with the return of RPI students housed in dorms directly across the street from the Troy High gym where the dances were held. Their return to campus created a bit of a problem, especially since some RPI students had begun infiltrating our dances the past several years.

The previous year there were several incidents where fights broke out between Troy High kids and the geek squads from RPI. They were horning in on our romantic prospects, with "Horn" being the operative word in this situation. Being horny teenagers ourselves, we found it very disturbing and disrespectful that these nerds, with their pocket protectors, fancy slide rules, protractors and high IQ's would have the nerve to invade our turf. Now their actions were creating a turf war.

The incident that really set things off was when Gary Spruce, a junior, watched his new girlfriend get hit on by a group of five, nerdy, future physicists, right before his eyes. He was incensed and wanted to defend his honor. However, he quickly realized that he was outnumbered and that these guys were much bigger than him. Faced with limited options and fearing that he might lose the affections of his latest crush to this gaggle of geeks, he quickly decided to call his brother. Gary's brother, Harry (Boo Boo) was a major league bruiser with a speech impediment. Harry was as tough as nails, stood about six foot two, and weighed about 230. Lucky for Gary, Harry only lived a few blocks from school and arrived at the scene on his bike within minutes to aid his little brother. Harry was usually very quiet and rarely lost his temper. But if he thought you were making fun of him or you disrespected his family or friends, he would turn into the jealous man in Jim Croce's "Big, Bad Leroy Brown" within seconds. Harry's reputation as a brawler was legend. Hence the nickname Harry Boo-Boo, If you messed with Harry, you got a boo-boo.

Billy, Larry and I had just arrived at the gym when we noticed a commotion near the south entrance.

"Who da fut do yuz think you are calling me Daffy Dut?" grumbled Harry. "Stop yur futtin laughing, or I'll kick yur asses all the way down to Pwospeck Paak!"

"Ha, ha, ha, ok, now the Troylet thinks he's a tough guy!" declared Levar, the biggest, brush-cut geek who was about the same size as Harry.

"Hey, wuh I say? Don't you dare call me a Twoylet," Harry bellowed. (Urchins, Troylets or any variation thereof were fighting words for many Trojans. Hum, I wonder if using that term was a reason for the ten year Trojan War in Homer's poem "The Iliad".)

"Oh boy, this is going to be great. These guys aren't going to know what hit them if they don't shut up," laughed Billy.

Well, to their chagrin, the RPI geeks stupidly didn't shut up or stop laughing at Harry. Instead, they continued their arrogant verbal assault, surrounded him and started pushing him, thinking that he wouldn't retaliate. Wrong! Soon pocket protectors, slide rules and brush-cut geeks were flying in every direction as Harry lowered their IQ's. Of course, the dance chaperones had already called the cops, and soon Harry was being wrestled to the ground and cuffed by four burly Troy cops. We last saw him being forced head first into a paddy wagon, as most of the Troy High kids cheered him on. He would forever be a folk hero in our eyes.

CHAPTER THREE

When Harry Met Charlie

Looking back now, I remember how I heard about Harry's reputation as a brawler and how I'd seen him riding his bike around town. I also heard the story from Billy Finch about the time a couple of grifters who had been hanging around the cobblestone alley next to the Famous Lunch tried to steal Harry's bike. Harry was sitting on the first stool at the lunch counter, scarfing down a dozen dogs and kibitzing with Charlie Coots and Billy when they heard a commotion coming from the alley. Sensing trouble, Harry lifted his hulking body off his frazzled stool and lumbered out the front door to see what all the yelling was about. Charlie and Billy followed him out.

Woodchuck, a harmless vagrant who often slept in the alley or the garbage dumpster stationed next to the Famous Lunch, was desperately scuffling with the grifters. They were trying to pry loose the Yale padlock Harry used to secure his bike to Woodchuck's sleeping quarters. Always plastered, you could never understand a word Woodchuck said. It always sounded like he was slurping a bottle of ripple from a paper sack. But Harry seemed to understand everything he was saying.

"Hey, leave him alone or I'll break yuz in two," bellowed Harry at these grizzly thieves.

"Give it your best shot, Bozo!" yelled the grimier looking grifter dressed in his grease- stained work pants and the rattiest looking plaid shirt you'd ever see. Harry saw red when he heard that dumb challenge. Within seconds, his nostrils began gushing copious clouds of super-heated steam. In a flash Harry grabbed this guy by the neck, twisted his right arm behind his back and slammed him head first into to the side of the dumpster. He then grabbed the smaller guy who was now trembling in fear and heaved him head first into that same stench- filled dumpster.

Home on a weekend pass from the United States Marines, Charlie was dressed in his freshly pressed service duds and brilliantly shined boots and stood in back of a growing crowd that had quickly assembled. "Way to go!" Charlie yelled.

"Kick him in the nuts before he gets back up," screamed Billy. Harry didn't notice that the little guy, now covered in lettuce, onion peels, carrot tops and decayed hamburger slime, was ominously hovering over his head, ready to whack him with a twisted two-by-four he retrieved from the dumpster.

"Watch out Harry, he's got a club!" screeched Vito Cerinelli, who seconds before had tossed his winning hand on the table in the back of Cohen's News Room (located directly across the alley) and rushed out to watch this battle. Sensing trouble, Harry immediately turned toward the dumpster just as this little runt swung that deadly lumber. Strong as an ox, Harry grasped it with the guy still attached to it and flung them both against Cohen's brick wall. The two-by-four snapped in two and the slimy runt collapsed in heap next to Woodchuck, who had resumed his normal station in life: sitting in a near stupor, legs splayed out in front of him and slurping on his half-filled bottle of ripple, oblivious to what was going on.

In the distance sirens began to wail as cops hastily flew down Congress Street to break up what they thought was a major melee after receiving an urgent call from an off-duty cop. Officer Bob Talrigio, who was having coffee at Manory's located just down the street from the Famous Lunch, had made the hasty call. Flashing his badge as he plowed through the crowd, he immediately came upon Charlie Coots, his past nemesis in earlier altercations. Charlie was innocently standing there and laughing along with Billy at this unfair epic battle.

"What are doing here, Coots?" demanded Officer Talrigio.

Ripping the cop's hand off his shoulder, Charlie quickly turned and saw that it was Talrigio. "What do you care what I'm doing here?" Charlie snarled back.

"Why you fucking weasel! You're probably AWOL," snapped Talrigio.

"Like hell I am," Charlie spouted back.

"Well you better get out of here or I'll haul your ass down to Central Station."

"Why? I ain't doing nothing but just standing here watching."

"That's it. I've had enough of your crap, move away, now!" Talrigio yelled, as he grabbed Charlie by the shoulders, pulled him out of the crowd and pushed him back towards Manory's, where a patrol car had screeched to a stop, blocking off both Congress and Fourth Street to traffic. A second car with its lights flashing and two front doors slung wide open blocked Congress Street in front of Cohen's. The officers had rushed into the alley with billy clubs in hand and began whacking Harry, who was kneeling on the first guy's chest pummeling him into oblivion. A third cop rushed to help subdue Harry because the first two weren't getting the job done cuffing Harry. During the midst of all of this Charlie started pushing back at Officer Talrigio because he was tired of being manhandled.

Talrigio had been waging a vendetta against Charlie ever since an incident at the Excelsior House on Snyder's Lake eighteen months earlier. Charlie had punched out Talrigio, who was off duty, plastered and an outright miserable drunk. He had begun badgering Charlie earlier while Charlie was having a good time with his buddies hitting on some pretty chicks at the bar. Apparently Talrigio had his sights set on one of those same chicks and thought Charlie was horning in. Talrigio initiated the fight but never got over Charlie cleaning his clock. He claimed Charlie had taken advantage of him because of his drunken condition.

So now, as one battle was ending, another was beginning—one that should never have occurred. Soon the crowd's attention became riveted on what was happening to Charlie as he tried to escape Talrigio's grasp in front of the glass door of Manory's.

"Let go of me," screamed Charlie. "You're messing up my uniform."

"I don't give a crap." Talrigio yelled back.

Suddenly Talrigio loosened his grip, and in the blink of an eye Charlie swung around, grabbed Talrigio's arm, and flung him through the front door of Manory's where he landed in a heap. Startled patrons screamed and dove for cover as shards of glass flew everywhere. Quickly the other cops subdued Charlie and then rushed to attend to their fallen comrade. Although he looked seriously injured, he only had a few superficial cuts on his arm. The worst injury was to his wounded pride—Charlie had whipped his ass again.

Charlie was slapped around pretty good that night in his holding cell at the police station. But in the morning Charlie's fuming station chief arrived at his arraignment, angrily demanding Charlie's release before City Court Judge Kasey. Kasey was a World War II veteran who served in Europe during the storming of the beach at Normandy. After hearing witnesses at the scene describe how Talrigio had instigated the altercation with Charlie, he dropped the charges of assaulting an officer and Charlie was released to his station chief's custody. However he had to pay for the broken window and his leave was canceled as punishment.

Harry Boo Boo's case was also dismissed after spending the night in the hoosegow. Apparently the two grifters he decimated had swiftly left town without filing charges. They knew there were outstanding warrants against them, ranging from petty larceny to grand theft auto.

CHAPTER FOUR

Booze, Drugs, Blackjack and Jail

Harry's brawling reputation didn't stop at the water's edge in Troy. It also encompassed the City of Albany. Harry lived in the Second Ward for several years as a young adult and often frequented the local watering holes. Harry was a heavy smoker with a few little quirks and superstitions. One of his quirks was the way that he removed cigarettes from his pack. On top of each cellophane-wrapped pack was a blue stamp that you had to remove in order to get at your cigarettes. Most people would just remove the wrapper, rip open the stamp and take out their cigarettes. Not Harry! Instead, he'd remove the wrapper and then meticulously open the pack from the bottom in order to get his cigarettes. That way he was able to preserve the stamp. (I guess Harry was a numismatist.)

One Friday night Harry was getting a bit tipsy at Nellie's Bar and Grill. Having consumed several pints of Hedrick's Golden Ale, Harry realized it was time to water the lilies. (Harry always used that expression when he had to take a leak.) Just as he was about to go to the john, a stranger plopped down next to him.

"How are ya doin?" he slurred to Harry.

"Good," Harry slurred back. "Watch my stuff, would ya, Wacket's?" (Wacket's was one of Harry's favorite salutations when greeting people. Harry thought everyone had some kind of racket.) When Harry returned, a couple of pints lighter, he noticed this stranger taking a cigarette out of the bottom of the pack. "Hey, what da futt you think you're doing, Wacket's?"

"What's it to you?" the stranger replied.

Bam! Harry whacked the guy and knocked him off his stool and onto the black and white tiled floor. Louie the bartender quickly ran to help other patrons pull Harry off this guy, without much success. Within minutes, four of Albany's finest were whacking Harry with their billy-clubs in a vain attempt to subdue him. Finally, one of the officers pulled out a black jack and opened Harry up. Harry's head was split wide open from the top of his right ear to his ear lobe. They were able to pull Harry, now groggy and bleeding profusely, off his unconscious prey. Both Harry and the cigarette pilferer were sent to the hospital to get stitched up. The stranger survived without any serious injury. But Harry was sent to the county jail for three days. Ironically, the cigarette pilferer wasn't really a pilferer. He just had the same quirk that Harry had. He was taking a cigarette out of his own pack, not Harry's. Harry had made a boo-boo!

Charlie Coot's, well he continued to manage to get into a brawl or two whenever he was home on leave from the service, usually down at the Riviera Club on the River Street strip. Carl Sargento used to work the door at the Riviera on weekends and often saw Charlie arrive three sheets to the wind. But this night was different. It was two am when Charlie appeared at the door and Carl immediately realized something was wrong. Charlie was incoherent, almost as though he was in some type of psychotic state, babbling unintelligibly as though he was having an out-of- body experience. If you touched his arm, he began flailing around as if he was punching an invisible ghost.

Carl quickly realized he had to get Charlie home before he went crazy and attacked some innocent patron he thought was attacking him in his "Bizarro World." Carl asked Chick Calsorino the bar manager if he could get Charlie out of there before all hell broke loose. Seeing Charlie's condition, Chick wisely agreed.

To get Charlie moving, Carl spoke to him softly then touched him gently on the shoulder. He then eased him into his car. With Charlie seemingly calm now, Carl quickly headed to Charlie's house, which was on the south side of State Street between Fourth and Fifth Avenues. As they approached the intersection at Fourth Street, Charlie became very agitated, started screeching, and tried to open the door while the car was moving. Luckily, Carl reached over, grabbed Charlie by the shoulder and held onto him until he was able to pull over to the curb. Carl then quickly raced around the side of the car and slapped Charlie across the mouth. Instantly Charlie came out of his drug-induced stupor, recognized Carl and calmed down.

Charlie's mom met them at the door then waved goodbye to Carl as she calmly walked Charlie into the house. Carl said that Charlie never remembered that night when he told him about it several weeks later while they were drinking at Walsh's Grill. To this day Carl swears someone slipped Charlie a mickey at some dive where he was carousing before showing up at the Riviera that night.

CHAPTER FIVE

The Lovely Maidens

When there were no dances at Troy High, we hopped on the Fifth Avenue bus and went to the Friday night dances at Catholic High in Lansingburg. In fact, that's where Billy met his girlfriend and future wife Rose Cullen. Billy became the first one in our group to actually have a girlfriend in high school. Larry and I became friends with some of Rose's school buddies who lived near Beman Park: Sue Gibby, her cousin Eileen Gibby, and Ellen Delahany.

We often hung out on their street or in Beman Park. When we first met them, we acted all goofy, like most young guys do when trying to get girls' attention. I usually just listened because I felt insecure and uncomfortable trying to tell jokes and stories, especially to girls. However, Larry was an excellent pitchman and had all kinds of lines and jokes. I, on the other hand, couldn't tell a joke to save my soul.

Larry and Billy occasionally went on double dates with Rose and Sue. Of course, I ended up staying home those nights, because I didn't have a date or the money to go on one. However, I did kind of like Sue. She was tall and pretty, even though she had a slight case of acne. She had a warm smile and nice personality and was always pleasant to me, even when I got up the courage to call her on the telephone. However, when I did call, she invariably developed an incredible urge to wash her hair, usually about five minutes into our conversation. I think she must have had an awful case of dandruff or something. One thing I know for sure, she had the cleanest hair in Beman Park. Besides being turned down by Sharon and brushed off by Sue, a series of incidents with girls created a template of emotional and hormonal frustration that I would unknowingly have to endure well into the future.

My neighbor and now freshman classmate, Tony Centannini, and I met two girls who lived in South Troy. Three days a week they attended the Mary Warren School, part of Holy Cross Episcopal Church located near the corner of Federal and Eighth Street. Maryanne was a pretty brunette about our age and her friend Diane Saberansky, an unattractive, dishwater blond, was her best friend and school mate. Of course, both Tony and I were attracted to Maryanne, especially me. However, as fate always seemed to dictate, Tony was the one whom Maryanne seemed more interested in.

We would meet them near Tony's house each afternoon and walk them all the way down to their houses on First Street near Monroe. The three of them would do most of the talking on this daily marathon-like trek, while I was an interested observer. I was so attracted to Maryanne. But she never realized it, because I was not the aggressive type that most girls seem to go for. As luck would have it, Tony and Maryanne dated all the way through high school, going to movies and major school dances and stuff.

I remember talking to my sister Brenda about wanting to have a date someday. She suggested that since I knew both Maryanne and her friend Diane that maybe I should call Diane to see if she might want to go to the movies with me—maybe we could double date with Tony and Maryanne.

So that Tuesday night after I came home from the Boys' Club, I finally got up the courage to call her. The call was brief and to the point: "Hi, Diane. It's Herbie. Would you like to go to the movies with me Saturday night?"

"Nope, I'm not interested."

"Uh, Ok. Thanks," I replied, stunned. "So, what's new?"

"Nothing; got to go."

"Bye," I said as I heard the phone click off. I was crushed. I didn't even care for her that much, and she wasn't even pretty. I was just so desperate to have a date.

"So what did she say?" Brenda asked excitedly.

"Not interested," I sighed.

"Don't be discouraged, Herbie. You'll get a date with someone nicer than her. I personally didn't care for her anyway."

"Neither did I, I thought she was kind of snooty. But it still hurts my feelings," I whined.

Finally an incident occurred later in my freshman year that I thought was going to be a turning point for me. Sue's friend Ellen Delahany, who lived around the corner on Eagle Street, was hanging out with us one warm spring night in front of Sue's house. Larry, Billy and I were laughing and busting each other's chops about who had the heaviest beard. I started shaving that year, even though you could barely see any whiskers on my chin. Luckily I found an old styptic pencil my father had left behind before he moved out and I was able to stop the bleeding each time I butchered myself shaving.

Rose, Sue and Ellen on the other hand were ignoring us and talking about what summer clothes they would be buying down at Denby's and which movies were playing at Proctors. That's when Ellen said she hadn't been to a movie in a long time because she was busy helping out at Saint Paul's, a Catholic Church on the Corner of Hutton Street. She and her family were devout Catholics and did fund raising events like Penny socials, bingo, and pot luck dinners to help out the church.

"Hey, you guys!" Ellen interrupted, pointing at us. "Why don't we go to the movies Saturday? I hear they are reshowing "King Creole". They say it's great."

Billy looked at Larry and smirked, "Sounds great, I missed that one, why don't you take Sue and I'll take Rose, and Herbie, um, maybe you can be Ellen's date."

I was flabbergasted at the awkward invitation Billy threw out. I peered sheepishly at Ellen, who was now silently staring at the sidewalk and digging at some dandelions in the cracks with her white sneakers, trying it seemed, to ignore what she just heard Billy say. Not sure exactly how to proceed, I quickly garnered the needed courage and blurted, "Ellen, would you mind going to the movies with me?"

She hesitated for what seemed an eternity then replied, "I'll go, but not as your date. I'll go as your friend." Even with this muted acceptance I was on cloud nine. I didn't know Ellen that well, but she seemed nice and was kind of cute in a plain sort of way. Now I would just have to come up with the money. So when I got home that night, I told Ma and she looked at me and smiled.

"You can go, Herbie. I made a few extra dollars this week from the pies and cakes I sold to Helen Howard for Walt's birthday last week."

"Thanks, Ma," I said. "you're the greatest!" So now I was going to go on my first 'official', unofficial date. We decided to go to the four o'clock show at Proctor's because Ellen's parents told her we could all come back to their house for soda and cake after the movie. I guess Ellen had also asked them if we could use their newly finished basement playroom after the movie. It had an old juke box, refrigerator and a ping pong table, along with a couple of couches and chairs to horse around on (I mean sit on). Ellen said her parents would be upstairs but promised to snoop on us to keep us out of trouble. Plus they didn't want us to be there late because she had to be up early for church.

When Saturday came I became distracted while watching my beloved, transplanted Dodgers on our second hand TV. I was totally engrossed watching my favorite players Duke Snider, Gil Hodges, Sandy Koufax on the Game of the Week. I didn't realize how late it was until Ma yelled.

"Herbie, weren't you supposed to go to the afternoon show at Proctor's?"

"Yea, Ma, the four o'clock show."

"Well, you better get your fanny moving. It's after three already."

"Holy crap," I thought to myself, "I better get moving or I'll screw up my first date." I had promised the guys I'd meet them all at the bus stop near Proctor's around three fifteen, so I rushed in and hugged Ma, who was standing at the sink washing the left-over lunch dishes. "Can I have the money for the movie now, Ma, please?"

She wiped her brow with a dish towel then reached into the tattered pocket of her apron and pulled out a crumpled five dollar bill and handed it to me. "That should be more than enough for everything, Herbie, Ok?"

"Ok, Ma. Thanks." I hugged her again as I raced out the door. I didn't bother to tell her I had found a buck and a quarter in coins under the couch and chair cushions in the parlor. I definitely had more than enough now for tickets, popcorn and sodas.

I was sweating like crazy as I raced down the RPI approach and headed west on Broadway. Just as I reached the corner near the Troy Record, I saw a bus pull up and a group of kids hop off near the post office a block away. They were laughing and looking around for someone as I waited patiently for the light to change. However, some impatient drivers blocked the walkway making it difficult for me to cross the street after the light turned.

By the time I finally got to the corner by the post office, I could see the group heading into the theater. One guy was tall, wore glasses, and looked something like Larry from a distance. Now I was worried that they had gone in without me because I had said I would be there earlier. I thought the Traction Company buses ran every fifteen minutes at least I hoped they did, because when I looked across Broadway into the huge window of the Chasan build-ing, the large clock on the wall read three twenty.

"Damn," I said to myself. "Did they leave without me?" I was getting really nervous now but decided that I would wait until the three thirty bus arrived just in case they were late. If they weren't on that one, then I would buy a ticket and look for them inside. I paced back and forth like an expectant father worrying that I'd screwed up my first date. "You freaking jerk!" I kept telling myself under my breath as each minute ticked by.

Peering down Fourth Street I saw a plume of black smoke billowing from what appeared to be a Traction Company bus in the distance. Breathing a shallow sigh of relief as the bus approached, I prayed they were on it. If they weren't, I would be devastated. It was exactly three thirty according to the clock in the Chasen Building, as the bus sputtered to an abrupt stop, spewing another plume of regurgitated pollutants. When the doors finally opened, several elderly ladies stepped onto sidewalk, followed by two young boys wearing Yankee baseball caps. After them came several RPI geeks in pinstripe shirts, with their obnoxious pocket protectors worn as status symbols, apparently to signify they were RPI students. They stood at the bus entrance arrogantly blocking other people from entering or exiting.

Within seconds I heard a familiar voice yell, "Move it, you don't own the sidewalk." It was Billy. He brushed the geeks aside as he, Larry, and the girls exited the bus and walked over to where I was standing. The stunned geeks looked on disdainfully, pondering what to do next, thought better of it and walked in the opposite direction. As we headed toward Proctor's, we could hear them in the distance yelling, "Troylets!" In unison Billy, Larry and I turned and yelled, "Assholes," and immediately flipped them the bird.

"Stop it, you guys. I don't like that kind of language," Ellen complained. "Be nice."

The three of us just smirked at each other and tried to ignore her, but Rose punched Billy lightly on the arm and sternly whispered to him. "Stop it, Billy. You know how religious she is. You apologize to her now."

"Yea, yea, I know. Sorry, Ellen." Billy chirped reluctantly.

It was then I figured I'd better apologize too since she was my date. "I'm sorry, Ellen. We got carried away because those RPI guys are always looking down their nose at us and insulting us. We have to stick up for ourselves."

"Well, that's still no reason to use foul language. We don't talk like that in my family. I hate hearing it."

"Sorry," I repeated with my head down. Now I was thinking this is not starting off the way I had hoped it would. I will have to be on my best behavior. When we got to the box office I told the lady, "Two tickets please." Immediately Ellen leaned forward and told the lady that she was buying her own ticket. I stood there in disbelief. I took my ticket, went inside the lobby and didn't know what to think or say. I soon realized I didn't have to say anything.

When Ellen came in, she walked up to me and said, "I told you the other night that we would go to the movie as friends and that I wasn't going to be your date."

"Well, uh, I thought I could at least buy your ticket," I stammered. "Can I at least buy you popcorn?"

"Thanks, but I don't feel comfortable with you doing that. But I will share the cost of a box with you and we can share it, Ok?"

"Ok." I was suddenly elated, at least for the moment. The rest of the afternoon was pretty uneventful except that Billy had his arm around Rose and Larry and Sue huddled whispering and laughing during the entire movie, while Ellen and I shared our popcorn in silence, each leaning awkwardly against the furthest side of our seats in order to avoid contact.

It seemed like Billy and Larry were both sort of making out, while all I could do was listen to Elvis singing those great Elvis songs "King Creole," "Trouble" and "Dixieland Rock." But even Elvis was sort of making out on screen with sleazy crook Maxie Field's floosy. I really didn't think I fit in with everyone that afternoon. I felt like an afterthought; that I didn't really belong with them and I kind of wished I never went. But then I thought, "Well, maybe things will be better when we go back to Ellen's house after the movie."

It was a bit chilly when the movie let out around seven. The sun was quickly setting as we shuffled onto the crowded bus, listening as our coins and tokens clanged and swirled around the metal and glass fare box dropping loudly into the coin vault. The bus was over crowded as we headed north along Fourth Street, so the driver didn't stop at all the bus stops. He even passed by the same geeks we had the run in with earlier who were now waving and yelling furiously for the bus to stop and pick them up. This time we just laughed and waved out the window at them as we passed by. They in turn gave us the finger which made us laugh even harder.

We all hopped off the bus at the corner of Fifteenth and Eagle and headed west toward Ellen's house, as the last golden strand of sunlight nestled gently beyond the horizon. When we entered Ellen's house, we were greeted by her mom, a petite woman with silver-brown hair, glasses and a welcoming smile. Behind her stood her husband, an average-sized fellow with reddish, gray hair and a reluctant, untrusting smile. I instantly thought this guy didn't trust us as far as he could throw us. Knowing how we acted at times, I couldn't blame him. I could tell he was very protective of his daughter and family.

We sat uncomfortably at the kitchen table and finished off their weekly family treat, a three layer vanilla, coconut, and cream-filled cake from Nelligan's Bakery. Then Ellen asked if we could all go down to their refurbished playroom to listen to music for a while. Her mom smiled and reiterated what she had told her earlier in the week that there would be no horsing around down there, as her husband hovered over the table with a stern look on his face. "We'll be good, Mrs. Delahany," Billy smirked. "Is it all right if we play some ping-pong ? "

"Sure, just be careful, please," she responded. "I don't want anyone to get hurt."

"No problem," Billy assured her.

"We can listen to music too, can't we, Mom?" Ellen asked.

"Yes, but not too loud."

We immediately headed down the tread worn stairs to their playroom. The room was large enough to house the ping pong table, but with little room to maneuver around it without banging into the walls. Of course, that's exactly what happened when Billy and I got into an epic battle. I hit a wicked forehand that Billy dove against the wall to get. He then drilled a backhand that forced me to dive head first into the couch that was occupied by the girls, as Larry stood by rooting us on.

"Stop it you guys before you wreck my house," Ellen yelled.

Within seconds, the cellar door flew open and there stood her father, his eyes glaring at Billy and me. "What is going on down here? It sounds like the walls are caving in."

"Sorry, Sir," I replied. "We were playing ping pong and Billy accidently tripped and fell into the wall. We will be more careful next time."

"There will be no next time," he stated, taking the paddles from us. "Ellen, they will have to leave if this continues. Do you understand?"

"Yes, Daddy, I understand. But can we please listen to the juke box a little while longer?"

With a disdainful look, he reluctantly agreed. "I will give you until ten o'clock then they have to leave. But if I hear anymore commotion before then, they're done, and you can never invite them back. Understood?"

"Yes, Daddy."

"Man," I whispered to Billy. "He doesn't take any crap, does he?"

"Ah, he'll get over it. Don't worry."

Billy and Larry then shoved their way onto the couch next to Rose, Susan and Ellen, while I plopped into an oversized arm chair adjacent to the couch. "Let's dance," Rose suggested, as Danny and the juniors warbled "At the Hop" on the juke box. Soon we were all up jitterbugging. It was such a blast bopping around the room with Ellen holding my hand as we danced. I actually was beginning to feel like we were connecting. We jitterbugged to a couple more songs when Larry reached over and turned the lights off when Pat Boon came on the juke box singing "Love Letters in the Sand". Ellen and I were now sitting on the couch watching, as Larry snuggled with Sue and Billy was kissing Rose while dancing. I looked at Ellen and asked if she wanted to dance. She looked at me and warily agreed. So I took her hand and moved onto the dance floor to join the others.

Now in my jaded mind I was super confident she liked me. We started slow dancing, sort of like old farts doing a Viennese waltz. I held her right hand in my left hand, which was slightly bent. I then put my right hand gingerly on her left hip and she immediately pulled back slightly, wary, I guess, about getting too close as she put her left hand on my shoulder. It felt very strange being so far apart. Especially since Billy, Larry and Rose and Sue seemed glued to each other's bodies.

When "I'm Mr. Blue" by the Fleetwood's came on I figured I would try to dance a little closer, like the others were doing. Well, that turned out to be a big mistake because when I took her right hand and held it against my chest and put my cheek next to hers, she pushed me away before I got anywhere near her boobs.

"What are you trying to do?" she blurted out so the others could hear.

"Nothing," I pleaded. "I was just trying to dance cheek-to-cheek like they're doing," pointing to Rose and Sue who were still glued to Billy and Larry.

"Well!" she said huffily, "I don't do that kind of dancing." That's when she pushed me away and turned the lights back on and told everyone it was time to leave. I think that kind of caught Larry and Billy off guard as they quickly attempted to cover the lumps in their kakis. As the girls grabbed their handbags to leave, Billy whacked me on the back of the head and said, "Thanks, Dip shit."

"Dip shit! Why'd you say that?" I impishly replied. "I didn't do nothing wrong. You guys were the ones making out, not me," I whispered as we scurried up the stairs and out the door before Ellen's father could give us the third degree.

This little, semi-amorous adventure was just another disaster in the date department for me. However, as it turns out, I shouldn't have felt so bad, because years later I learned Ellen became a nun. God bless her and me because she definitely gave all the warning signals, but I was too young and naïve to realize it. However one question lingered in my mind when I found out she became a nun: Did I drive her into the nunnery? So instead of girls, I tried to keep my focus (not always successfully) on sports, art and music which became a big part of my life for three years.

CHAPTER SIX

A Change, of Course

High school was a big change for me. We had started changing classrooms in grade school for each subject, and I was used to it. Now I had to adapt to a new group of teachers: some interesting, some boring, a few eccentric. My homeroom teacher Mrs. Rogers was a sweetheart and reminded me of my fourth grade teacher, Mrs. Grantham. However, she wasn't quite as old and didn't fall asleep like Mrs. Grantham did. She was a bit matronly looking though, which in a way was comforting to me.

I also had new classmates to deal with, which would become a challenge, especially the girls. Luckily there were a few hold-over classmates from grade school: Georgia Holland, Jim Polacheck and several others, including, of course, Larry, Billy and Ronnie. However, Larry and Billy were assigned to other homerooms, while Ronnie remained with me along with a new kid named Rocky Stewart. I was assigned to sit in the middle of the row next to the window right in back of a beautiful, brown-haired girl named Margie and across from her best friend Sandy. They apparently had been friends since grade school. Right in back of me was a thin, dark-haired girl named Terry who was very athletic and loved to talk. She and I became sort of good friends but not in a romantic way. She loved sports like me and would become one of the youngest varsity cheerleaders in school history.

Each morning there were PA announcements made by the principal or some other minion assigned the boring task on days he wasn't able to make them. We always recited the Pledge of

Allegiance with our hands held over our hearts, and there was no outcry about the word "God" being included during this non-politically-correct era.

My first class of the morning was Miss McGonigal's art class. She was tall and thin with her hair usually up in a bun. However, she dressed very well, usually wearing earrings, a necklace and stylish glasses; somehow she had the look of a dowager about her. I had heard rumors that she was a tough teacher. However, I found her to be very nice, although a bit stern about making sure we finished our projects on time. I learned a lot about perspective and composition in her class.

We did some poster work my freshman year but her expertise was in teaching painting techniques, mostly in water color. I liked water color and was pretty good at it. But one of my classmates, Al Cocco, was so far ahead of me in technique and talent. Al and I became casual friends in art class. Just watching him and his techniques helped me to improve my skills over time. Seeing his terrific work took some of the swelling out of the inflated ego I had brought to high school from grade school. I was subconsciously learning a valuable lesson. The further you advance in life, the tougher the competition becomes. There will always be someone better than you, but if you strive to be the best you can be—then you will be successful.

Art was one of my favorite subjects in high school along with gym and biology. Al ended up doing a lot of the art work and design for our class year book. From what I have been told, Al attended the University of Rochester, majoring in art, graduated at the top of his class, and at one point in his career headed the Art Department at the University.

The best thing I remember about Miss McGonigal's class was when she selected me and a few others in class to participate in a national poster contest to honor the United Nations. Karla, Al and I won honorable mention for the northeast region of the country.

Other than that award, nothing extraordinary happened to me in my art classes. However, I discovered that I really loved art and sports and thought early on of becoming an art teacher and a coach. That is if I didn't become a world famous athlete or artist first.

Bulletin: None of those things happened, yet. Hey, maybe I'll become a famous humorist instead and sign my books using my initials—HAH. People might get a chuckle out of that.

CHAPTER SEVEN

Ivan Who and Study Hall Drama

My second class on Monday, Wednesday and Friday was gym, and on Tuesday and Thursday it was study hall. One of the three gym days was actually swimming class. Troy High had an excellent varsity swimming and diving team. But unlike grade school, guys were given the option of wearing bathing suits in high school. However, I think they had to wear them during swim meets. Swimming classes were much more intensive and we actually learned all the different strokes and safety techniques in the Olympic-sized pool. Some of the better swimmers graduated to lifeguard classes where they learned survival techniques. I loved watching them during their training sessions when they had to jump in the pool fully clothed, then remove those clothes and turn them into air-filled floatation devices.

The most boring yet at times fun class was third period English. It was taught by an eccentric yet funny old lady every kid talked about. She looked rather unkempt with her wrinkled print dresses and scuffed black shoes. Her thinning hair was pulled into a tight bun that failed to capture illusive strands of gray that meandered aimlessly in every direction. She always kept her glasses propped firmly on top of her head, highlighting even further her burgeoning bald spot and the hearing aids she had in each ear.

To her credit, she certainly tried to make Shakespeare tolerable through her dramatic readings and acting out like an inspired thespian. She was a tough but fair teacher. She badgered us to read and like "Ivanhoe," then assigned a five page paper as part of our first semester exam. I struggled to write that paper, especially with an eye to correct grammar. I got a C+ along with lots of colorful red reminders about my grammatical ineptitude. (I have an editor now who has the same red pencil, thank God!)

The funniest day I ever remember in her English class was when she was reading a verse from "Ivanhoe." Dick Cross, one of our class clowns, was sitting in the aisle seat next to the storage room at the back of the class. He was making wise cracks about how she was going bald. Sandy Naylor, a shy, blond beauty was trying to hold back a laugh when out of the blue comes Mrs. Fauxwald. She was hopping down the aisle like a Templar knight, riding her horse into battle. In her hand was a sharpened pencil facing out like a jousting lance, and she immediately (accidentally?) stuck Dick in the forearm, drawing a shriek and little blood.

"What the hell is the matter with you, you crazy old witch!" Dick shouted while grasping his arm. "Why did you stab me?"

"I didn't stab you," she exclaimed. "It's your own fault for sticking your arm out in the aisle. Besides, you know the rules—no talking in my class. I may have a little trouble hearing, but I could hear you out on Burdett Avenue. Now go down to the nurse and get that cleaned out. When you come back, take your chair into the storage room and sit there until class is over!"

One of the weirdest and scariest things that ever happened to me in high school occurred in a study hall near the auto-body shop. It was a long narrow room with no windows and only one exit door. Outside the door was a long hallway lined with windows. Without the light from those windows study hall would have felt like a dungeon. There was occasional horseplay but not too much. I think that was because it was right after lunch and we were all a bit tired. I was actually reading my homework assignment for a change when all of a sudden I heard a loud screech and a horrible thud several rows away. Dave Strockman had fallen on the floor and was flailing around uncontrollably. The study hall teacher was nowhere to be found when I reached David. I remembered hearing that if a person was having an epileptic seizure that he could swallow his tongue and choke to death. I had also heard stories that you could put a pencil or ruler in the person's mouth. However, I had neither with me as I knelt over him and Susan melnick continued to scream.

Instinctively, and stupidly, I reached into his mouth and held his tongue, thinking I would save him from either choking to death or biting off his tongue. With all the adrenaline running through me now, nothing mattered to me. He was slobbering all over my hand by the time the nurse came and luckily pulled my hand away. It was really stupid doing what I did because he could have bitten a finger off. But it was a dire situation, so I did what I did, stupid or not. The only saving grace of this traumatic event was that we realized David had a problem no one ever knew about, and that Susan later told me what I did was one of the bravest things she had ever seen. I'm not sure it was bravery, but for whatever reason I knew I had to act or something horrible might have happened to him.

CHAPTER EIGHT

What's the Deal with Football?

Tommy Fitch and I signed up for freshman football. Both of us had played touch football for School 14 with Frankie Vumbaco and Cookie Lombardo in seventh and eighth grade. But now being freshman, we could finally play tackle. In grade school we were only allowed to play touch football. Yet the Catholic schools allowed brain-rattling tackle football. Go figure. I was envious watching Denny Barrow playing tackle football for St Francis in the mud and slop at Prospect Park the previous fall. Playing in sloppy weather was so much fun. You would get all dirty and slimy, yet rarely got hurt. Except of course me!

In late November of eighth grade, Tommy and I were able to get into a pickup game at Northfield on the RPI campus. It was the night before the big RPI-Union game. The RPI team had just finished a late afternoon practice under the lights and the field was all chewed up and muddy from a torrential downpour earlier in the week. There were about twelve guys playing a modified game of tackle, including some guys from the RPI fraternity next door. It was so fun. I played halfback and wide receiver while one of the frat guys was quarterback, and Tommy played linebacker on the opposite team. Of course, no one wore pads or equipment.

I had a couple of decent runs from my halfback position. Jason, the quarterback, called a play in the huddle for me to run a post pattern deep. There were only a few minutes left to play before the lights were to be shut off so we had to run our plays quickly. We were down by one point, having missed an extra point conversion earlier. At the snap count, I made a fake to my right, then zig-zagged toward the end zone with Tommy in hot pursuit. I saw the ball sailing toward my outstretched hands and dove to make the catch. I caught the ball in full flight, just as Tommy landed on my back, knocking the ball loose. His crushing tackle forced me to slide head first into the slop with my hands outstretched to protect myself.

My left hand was searing with pain as Tommy finally got off me. Looking down I could see a muddy pulp on the palm of my hand. Tommy asked me what happened. Now sitting up and in grinding pain, I showed him my hand. "Boy, that's a mess! Let me see if I can clean out some of that crud." He returned shortly with a dirty towel he had dunked into a water bucket and began rubbing my hand in an effort to extract the ground-in dirt that was just under the skin in my now bleeding hand.

"Stop, Tommy!" I yelled. "It hurts too much and you got most of it out anyway."

"Ok. I was just trying to help."

"I know. Thanks. I'll have Ma clean it out when I get home." However, instead of going right home after the game we stopped by the grocery store near the corner Eighth and Federal Streets for a soda and Snicker's bar. We bullshitted for a while on the weather-beaten brownstone steps of Megan's store. My hand was barely hurting me by the time I got home. But being an air head, I forgot to tell Ma about the injury until close to bedtime, when it started aching again.

Ma looked at me in disbelief, shook her head and said, "Herbie, Herbie, Herbie, what am I going to do with you?" She then whipped out the peroxide and tried her best to clean out the residual gunk that Tommy never got out. However, like what happened when I impaled the sliver in my foot as a little kid, this trauma would end up with me in the hospital emergency room. By Sunday night I had developed a high fever and my hand was now red and swollen. My sister Dorothy brought me to St. Mary's Hospital. However, instead of getting a shot of penicillin and being sent home, this time I was admitted.

I was deathly sick in the emergency room and puked my guts up every few minutes into a kidney shaped metal pan. I was immediately put on a course of antibiotics in hopes of stopping the infection from spreading before they sent me upstairs to a four-person ward. However, after a night of constant vomiting and a high fever, they decided to bring in a surgeon. Dr. Sappihosa was short, had slanted eyes, and spoke broken English I could barely decipher. He looked like a Japanese fighter pilot in pale blue coveralls and surgical mask. I was able to decipher that he was going to operate and drain the puss that was spewing out of my hand.

"Here we go again," I thought, as I remembered getting my tonsils out as a kid. "It's going to be pain, ether, vomit, pain, ether, vomit, ice chips, and ice cream." However, when I woke up this time there was no Mom, ice chips or ice cream. I was still so nauseous that I vomited for several more hours as they pumped IV fluids into me. When I finally started coming around later that afternoon, my hand was throbbing from the surgery. It was wrapped in sterile gauze with a drainage tube sticking out that was emptied periodically by a nurse. She also gave me some pills to quell the pain. The next day I was given a sponge bath, back rub and had my bandages changed. I also began eating soft foods. I was in the hospital one whole week to ensure the infection was totally out of my system. I remember Dorothy coming back to pick me up for the cab ride home. It was unusually warm that early December day. The ice and snow that had cloaked the many trees lining Eighth Street from an early winter storm were finally beginning to shed their wintery coats. Tiny chunks of ice clanged off the roof of our cab as we neared my house.

Who would have thought a seemingly simple injury to my hand would bother me for over a year. But it did. Although it appeared to heal quickly from the outside, the surgery must have nipped a nerve in my wrist because it was extremely sensitive to the touch, especially when playing basketball at the Boys Club that year. Eventually it did clear up, but in the meantime, every time I got slapped on the wrist or it was hit by errant pass, I would immediately get sick to my stomach. Luckily, I never puked my guts up on the court.

CHAPTER NINE

A Strapping Jock

When we reported for our first official Troy High football practice in September, we practiced with no contact. We just did lots of running and calisthenics for the first four days. On Friday they handed out gear that looked like a throwback to the 1930s. We were given used black leather football shoes that had hard white plastic and metal cleats. They were smelly from years of built up sweat and fungus that had seeped into the leather. In addition, there were not enough hard plastic helmets to go around, so some guys had to wear old, dilapidated, brown leather helmets that, unlike the newer ones, lacked a plastic face guard. Although the newer ones were supposed to protect your face, they rarely did. Stray fingers, knuckles and fists often hit their mark in a pile-up resulting in scrapes, bruises, gouges and chipped teeth. The shoulder pads I was given were so big they hung out a couple inches off my shoulders with my scrawny arms hanging out like little sticks from my oversized practice jersey.

After practice we would get more equipment: pants with built in thigh pads, rubberized hip pads and in some cases replacement chin straps that didn't come with our original helmets. The one piece of equipment I didn't have was a jock strap (athletic supporter) that I saw most guys wearing after our first practice. I always wore my boxer shorts to practice. Aside from getting laughed at by my "macho" new teammates for not wearing one, I got chewed out by the coach that Friday when he found out. During all my years of playing little league baseball, I never realized that I should have been wearing one for my own manly protection. Looking back, I could have had some serious injuries if I took a hit to the family jewels.

"Listen, Hydie," Coach Manelli yelled, "You better not come back to practice without one, or you won't be playing football. Hear me?"

"Yes, sir." I timidly responded. Then I thought to myself, "Where the hell am I going to find one of those contraptions?" I might have to quit football before I even get started. I was so sad and bedraggled as I dawdled my way home <u>that</u> evening with Jimmy Roscoe, a blond-haired freshman like me, who lived in the Ahearn apartments. Jimmy was vying for the same quarterback slot as me.

"Geez, Jimmy. How I'm going to be able to get a jock strap before the next practice on Monday?"

"I don't know. My Dad bought me one when I was in little league and It still fits."

"What! They come in different sizes?" I innocently blurted.

With a look of disbelief on his face Jimmy laughed, "Of course they do. You think that little pecker of yours isn't going to grow as you get older?"

"Hum," I said to myself. "I never thought of that, and how did he know what me pecker looked like anyway?" We soon parted ways as he headed down toward Congress Street and I headed up Eighth to my house, waving to Ronnie Moore as I passed the store.

"Well, Herbie, how was your first week of practice? I see you're still in one piece." Ma joked. She was really concerned that I'd get hurt because I was still so tiny.

"It went ok," I said, not wanting to divulge all the details of how the guys laughed at me for not wearing a jock strap. Plus, if I didn't get one, I wouldn't be allowed to play. I was in a dilemma. How could I tell my Mom I needed a jockstrap? She probably never heard of such a thing. I was sure she didn't.

I was very quiet at supper, hardly saying a word as I slowly probed Ma's baked macaroni. A sure sign I was distracted because usually I would have gobbled down my first helping and would be begging for more. "Ok, Herbie. What's the matter? You're too quiet. Something is bothering you. What is it?"

"Nothing's bothering me, Ma," I lied.

"Don't lie to me, I know something is wrong. You're normally on your second helping by now. Are you sick? Did you get hurt at practice?" Boy, now I was in a predicament. How could I tell her? "Herbie answer me, or you're not going to Beman Park tonight."

"Come on, Ma, that's not fair," I whined.

"Oh, yes it is," she said, beginning to raise her voice. She knew me inside and out when I was sick, when I was trying to finagle something and when I wasn't telling the whole truth.

"Geez," I thought, "I've got to tell her now because I was really wanted to hang out with Billy, Larry and Ronnie...Ok, Ma. I didn't want to tell you because I didn't know if you would understand. The coach told me that if I don't get a jock-strap, I can't play football. Do you know what that is, Ma?"

"Uh, yea, Herbie, I've heard of them," Ma said with a wry smile on her face. "But you should call them what they are, athletic supporters."

"Ok, Ma." I said. Dumbfounded she'd heard of those contraptions. "Hey, Ma, how did you know what they are?"

"Well, Herbie, you're not my only son. Your brother Sonny used one when he was playing baseball for the National Guard. In fact, I still have it somewhere. I'm sure he wouldn't mind if you took it since he's getting married soon and spends most of his time working at the fire department."

"Thanks, Ma, you're a life saver. Can I go to the park now?"

"Yes, Herbie, you can go."

That Monday I went into the boys' locker with my spanking new (used) jock-strap. I had seen Ma pack it, along with my other gym stuff into the used duffle bag Sonny had given me at the start of the school year. It was pure white with Ma having bleached it the night before. Just as I was about to get dressed for practice the coach stuck his head out of his office and yelled to me.

"Hey, Hydie, did you get that jock-strap?"

"Yes, Sir," I yelled back while proudly holding my jock-strap in the air. However, when I put it on, it didn't exactly fit tight and felt very rough around the edges as though Ma had starched it. Luckily it fit just tight enough that my private parts didn't fall out from the excessive room they were exposed too.

Although we rarely played against the varsity in practice, we did learn a lot about the basics of football during that fall. On occasion Coach Picken, the varsity coach, would pick out one of the bigger kids to practice a couple of the varsity plays. He usually picked Jimmy Rosco or Lee Bennett. Although I didn't play in any actual games that year, I learned how to block, throw passes and run the ball. I also got myself into pretty good shape physically. We were also allowed to watch the varsity scrimmage, but weren't allowed to dress for those games.

One scrimmage game in particular sticks out in my mind. I remember how big all the kids looked. Dick Sullivan was a real bruiser at linebacker; he stood about six feet tall and weighed nearly 210 pounds. Ralph Pagano was a brute at tackle, standing about six foot two and 235 pounds. We all thought he was tough as nails on the field. His dad, Ralph senior, would attend most afternoon practices and all the scrimmage games. He owned a painting business and always found time to watch his son play. A former player himself, he was demanding and tough with his kids from what I heard.

We were playing Cardinal McClosky that Tuesday afternoon. It was a very physical game because both teams hated each other. Our quarterback Arnie (Giggi) Manderville had been sacked a couple times, and I could hear Ralph's Dad screaming at Ralph for missing his block which resulted in a sack. Ralph hobbled off the field bent way over and holding his arm. However, his Dad continued to harangue from the sideline. All of a sudden young Ralph collapsed on the ground screaming and cradling his arm. His Dad continued to scream at him while Ralph was crying in pain and writhing on the ground. "Stop your damn crying, Ralph. Be a man!"

"Stop it, Ralph." Coach Picken angrily yelled at Ralph senior. "Can't you see he's injured?" Quickly, Chuck Howland, the soccer coach who was watching the scrimmage, and Gene Barman, our gym teacher, rushed to Ralph's side. It became clear that this was no minor injury. I could see young Ralph's arm, and it seemed that a piece of bone was protruding and blood was streaming onto the ground. Richie Armao, who played half-back for the varsity, as well as Giggi, Dickie Sullivan, Freddie Case and several others huddled around their wounded teammate. They looked on in shock, having never seen such an ugly injury before. I hadn't either and began to wonder, do I really want to play this sport?

CHAPTER TEN

Friday Night Duh-lights!

Although I didn't get to play an actual game during my freshman year, I still loved to go to them, especially when we played on Friday nights at Hawkin's Stadium in Menands. Billy, Larry and I crowded onto the Traction Company bus that would spirit us to Menands and the big game with Charlie Leigh and the Albany High squad. We had heard the outlandish, urban legend that Charlie was actually a grown man, 23 years old, and had played for six years on this juggernaut of a team. (He *was* that good and actually played in the NFL several years later.)

The excitement of Friday night lights engulfed us as we stumbled off the crowded bus and pushed our way through the ancient metal turnstiles in front of this iconic stadium where Babe Ruth once played an exhibition game. The game was just about starting as we exited the gangway leading to the stands. Brilliant lights lit up the emerald green grass and iron red dirt infield where the football field was marked off in white lime dust. Just as we headed up to the top of the stadium where the best seats were located, we were bombarded by paper airplanes sailing over our heads, heading toward the field and exploding in mid-flight by the home made firecrackers Luke Robert's brother Jeff had made for the occasion. Paper shrapnel floated down on us as each paper airplane exploded, setting off a staccato of laughs and screams from unsuspecting kids below. Of course, we all laughed our asses off because we had heard that Jeff had made up these special missiles for the game. (Jeff was a few years older than us and was a chemistry major in college.)

He almost got us in trouble later that fall when somehow one of his home-made fire crackers exploded inside a US Postal mail box. We didn't put it there, but we did manage to explode one in a telephone pole a block away earlier that night. No one ever found out who actually put one in the mail box. But, I am definitely sure it wasn't us. I am also positive I didn't put the one in the telephone pole. I won't say who did because I don't remember, I developed amnesia that night from all the explosions.

However, I do remember so many other stupid things that we did as teenagers like the time later that fall when we all headed up to Lilly's ice cream shop on upper Congress Street. We had packed onto the Albia bus in front of Denby's around nine o'clock on Friday night. Somehow Billy, Larry and Ronnie had gotten hold of a few packs of Chinese firecrackers some guy was selling to kids near Front Street. Several kids were lighting them and throwing them in the air to explode over people's heads. Their timing had to be perfect in order to accomplish their mission: scare shoppers half to death without injuring them or themselves.

As we were getting on the bus, some kids would laugh as they described jumping out of the way just before one blew up near their feet. I didn't think it was too funny at the time and was chided by the guys for not taking part in their stupid and dangerous prank. I remembered back to the story Alan had told me about the time one of his friends lost part of his finger when playing with dynamite caps and cherry bombs down by the train station. All the guys knew how dangerous dynamite caps were, Alan said. But apparently they didn't realize cherry bombs were just as bad. Gary Mason, his friend, was alone one day taking turns setting off stolen dynamite caps by throwing bricks at them, then lighting cherry bombs and throwing them down the tracks to explode out of harm's way just around the corner from Gaynor's Gay Spot. He thought he was safe in a secluded gang-way off Sixth Avenue. However he wasn't so lucky, because as he was about to throw his last cherry bomb, it suddenly exploded just as it was leaving his outstretched hand.

He was writhing in pain and bleeding profusely when the cops came. They had received reports of shots being fired or explosions just a stone's throw from central station. Although Gary got into some serious trouble for what he did, he was actually lucky that he got caught. Because if the cops hadn't come who knows what might have happened to him; he could have bled to death. That story always stuck in my mind.

All the way up Ferry and Congress Streets, Billy, Larry, Ronnie and other kids would light these tiny firecrackers and throw them out the open windows of this packed bus. "Come on, Herbie, take one!" Billy implored.

"Na, I don't feel like it."

"What are you, chicken shit?" one smart mouth kid I didn't know yelled over at me.

"Screw you," I yelled back. My temper was beginning to roil at this stupid jerk I didn't know.

Just as I was about to get up and smack this kid for challenging my masculinity and courage, the bus jerked to a sudden stop. Luckily Ronnie grabbed me before I could get to this doofus who was about four inches taller and thirty pounds heavier than me.

"Don't waste your time, Herbie," Ronnie said. "He isn't worth it." However, I was still pissed and asked Ronnie if he had any firecrackers left. He had one and gave it to me. I was so upset with this guy that I was going to throw it at him.

"Give me a light, Larry, hurry" I implored.

Larry lit the end of my little firecracker, and I was poised to hurl it at this clown who was across the street and almost out of range. Just as my arm moved forward, I heard a loud explosion in my right ear and a burning sensation in my fingers. The damn thing exploded in my hand just like Alan's friend's had. Luckily mine was just a tiny Chinese firecracker and not a cherry bomb. My ears rang for two days and my fingers had minor burn blisters on them. I guess I should have taken better heed of Alan's story. It seems vanity and acting out of vengeance is not always the best policy.

CHAPTER ELEVEN

Eggs Are No Yoke

Another stupid incident occurred on Halloween. I was now too old to actually go trick-or-treating with my sisters anymore, so I decided to go downtown for some excitement. As little kids, we didn't do anything but go door-to-door throughout our local neighborhood and what was known to us as the rich people's neighborhood up by Boughton Road, Tibbett's Avenue and Burdett Avenue. We heard rich people always gave out better stuff, which turned out to be false. We usually got better candy from our own neighbors. Plus some of the rich people could be pretty snotty to us. They asked us where we lived and when we told them, they closed their doors in our face as though we had the bubonic plague or something worse—we were one of those Troylets! I think that may have been the reasons why Alan, Billy and the older guys used to egg their houses or spray them with shaving cream. I was never allowed to hang out on Halloween with the older guys because Ma feared they would teach me their bad habits and one delinquent per family was enough.

I was downtown near the Frear Building when I ran into this older kid I had seen at high school. His name was Tom Chapleman and he lived in Sycaway. He was a junior I'd see horsing around the cafeteria once in a while. He was a red head with a slight case of acne, which gave him a ruddy complexion. He and his buddies were usually picking on a developmentally disabled kid they had nicknamed Digger the dummy. I think his dad worked at one of the local cemeteries. They would take his lunch bag away and force him to recite the alphabet frontward and backward which he couldn't do and then laugh at him. Other times they forced him to do hand-stands. Those jerks would get their jollies at his expense before giving his lunch back.

I had started the night by stopping at Woolworths because I heard they were handing out free candy. Plus, I could take a ride on the escalator which was the first in the area. Several stores in the city gave out candy as a way of stemming kids' urges to egg or spray shaving cream on their windows. But that didn't always work because some kids were just plain nasty, no matter how well they were treated.

I think this kid just had a nasty streak in him. I was just about to head home for the night when I saw him in the alley peering around the Frear Building. He had a can of shaving cream in one hand and an egg in the other. "Psst, hey, you," he whispered as I walked by. "Are there any more cops on the corner?"

"I don't know." I said. "I wasn't paying any attention. Why?"

"Well, they picked up a couple of my buddies earlier for egging the Gordon L. Hayes store."

"So why are you guys doing stuff like that?" I asked.

"We do it because it's fun; except when you get caught, and I ain't never been caught."

"It doesn't look like much fun to me," I said.

"Come on," he laughed. "It is fun. I got an extra can of shaving cream in my coat pocket you can use. You won't get caught, I never do. You just have to run fast and know the right hiding places."

"Not tonight." I said. "I'm heading home."

"Well, you don't know what you're missing." With that I waved good bye and headed home with a bag full of candy to munch on. Ironically I learned the next day that the dork who never gets caught and who picks on developmentally disabled kids got caught! He ended up in juvenile court for vandalism and he deserved it.

CHAPTER TWELVE

Catch a Fleeting Star

Along with playing football and basketball, I also played fresh-man baseball that spring along with continuing to play Babe Ruth baseball during the summer. Gene Delvecchio was my fresh-men baseball coach and I learned a lot from him. I remember bat-ting 400 that year. Of course, we only played about ten games, so a 400 average wasn't anything spectacular. But I did have several triples and one inside the park home run at Prospect Park. They didn't have fences at the big diamond so you didn't have to hit it over a fence to get a home run. Being so thin and quite fast for a little guy, I was able to quickly round the bases after hitting the ball over the center fielder's head. He got to the ball just before it neared the road. But by then I was already rounding third base. That'll teach him for doubting my "tremendous power' and playing such a shallow center field.

I wasn't quite Babe Ruth, but I did have one home run in grade school, little league, high school and Babe Ruth League, that inside the park home run. However, the ones in grade school and little league were "monster drives" which barely made it over the fence. The summer after my freshman year was my last playing Babe Ruth baseball. I alternated playing center field and second base for Arbit Furniture that year and in addition even pitched a few innings. The highlight was when I struck out Bobby Weaver. I think I shocked the world when I did because it rarely happened. I remember Bobby walking away from the plate shaking his head in disbelief and probably thinking: "How the hell did that happen?

Scrawny Herbie Hyde just struck me out?" He looked totally con-fused because it was so rare and I really wasn't a pitcher.

Our Babe Ruth All Star team consisted of many of the same kids I played with in Little League, plus some new kids. Just as we did in Little League, we won all our preliminary games and were now playing for the district championship in Schenectady. We had been beating most teams quite comfortably during the prelims. I was a second stringer and rarely played except as a pinch runner. I was pretty fast and actually scored a couple runs in the tourna-ment. As usual, Bobby Weaver was hitting towering home runs in every game, as well as pitching a couple one hitters. When he wasn't pitching, a tall kid name Jimmy Maloney usually pitched for us while Tony Yates or Tag Dement might come in relief. I had pitched a couple times for a few innings during regular season games and had a good fast ball.

I would ride to most of the away games with Tag Dement and his father along with several other players. We knew the champion-ship game was going to be a tough one because Schenectady had a powerful team too. Our game was scheduled for 2:30 that Saturday and Tag's dad was supposed to pick me up around 12:30. Since I hadn't eaten lunch yet, I decided to open a can of potted meat Ma had in the cupboard. I hoped a couple of sandwiches would hold me over until after the game. I was really hungry even though I had already eaten a large breakfast a few hours earlier.

Back in those days some cans had little metal keys to open them up. However, if you weren't careful you could get nasty cut from them. Well, I wasn't careful and sliced the index finger of my throwing hand. Not great timing to get a nasty cut on game day. Boy, it hurt like hell. When Ma heard me screech, she rushed into the kitchen to see what happened. "Herbie, how many times have I told you to be careful opening those cans?" Ma said, as she shook her head in disbelief.

"I know Ma, it was stupid," I replied honestly.

I then had to go to the sink and hold a dishcloth on my finger until Ma got some peroxide and a couple bandages. It was bleeding pretty badly and I was beginning to fear I might have to get stiches and miss the game. After holding the wash cloth for several minutes, the bleeding seemed to have subsided somewhat by the time Ma took off the cloth and rinsed my finger with peroxide. "Oh shit, oh shit that stings," I whined when the peroxide hit the cut. It almost felt as bad as when I got cut.

"Watch your mouth and stop acting like a baby, Herbie," Ma yelled, "or I won't let you go to the game."

After Ma held my finger for about ten minutes and put the bandage on, the bleeding finally stopped. But my finger was still extremely sore by the time Mr. Dement arrived. When we got to the field and started our pre-game practice, I could barely hold the ball because it hurt so much. However, it didn't hurt too badly during batting practice. I could grip the bat fairly comfortably but gripping the baseball remained a problem.

Schenectady had a well groomed field, a huge scoreboard in center field, and newly painted wooden bleachers that ran along both baselines. The stands were full and people lined the outfield fence. Bobby was embroiled in a pitcher's duel with a lanky right hander by the name of Ed Barnowski who would go on to pitch for a couple years in the Baltimore Orioles organization. We had eked out a couple infield hits and had pulled within a run with a sacrifice fly, but were still behind two to one going into the bottom of the sixth inning. Bobby would be up third in the top of the seventh if were we able to get out of this inning without giving up any more runs. He was overdue to hit another home run.

Bobby's arm was beginning to tire and Coach William's felt he had to pull him before we got into more trouble. So he looked down the bench to see who he could put in to get that final out. Unbelievably he pointed to me to go in and pitch.

"Me?" I thought to myself, "Why, me?"

He didn't want to put in Jimmy Maloney if he didn't have to, because he had pitched the previous game and really wanted to save him for the regionals if we won today. "Herbie, come here," Coach Williams said. "We know you have one of the best fastballs in the league and we want you to go in and just throw strikes. Can you do that?"

I was stunned and nervous but I had to tell the coach the truth. "Coach, I don't think I can do it with this finger." I pleaded, pointing to the blood stain bandages. "It really hurts when I grip the ball. But it doesn't hurt when I grip the bat for some stupid reason." I really thought he'd be mad at me but he wasn't. He had been trying to play me more often lately which made me feel good, but I would have hated to cost us the game by lobbing up a bunny that someone would knock over the fence.

Luckily, he decided to put in my friend Tony instead. Tony was a much better pitcher than I could ever be and had one of the sneakiest, slowest curve balls I ever faced. He struck me out on that damned thing more times than I care to remember.

Coach knew he had to keep Bobby (our best hitter) in the game. So instead of removing him, he took out Jack Klasdi, our catcher, instead. Bobby took his place behind the plate. Making those changes would insure that Bobby would get another crack at Barnowski. Coach was hoping Bobby would come across for us with his bat in the last inning. So with men on second and third, two outs, and the count at three and two, Tony slowly wound up and unleashed the slowest drop ball I had ever seen. The poor batter never had a chance as it glided like the Hindenburg over the plate, then dropped off the face of the earth just as the batter swung. He swung so hard that he missed it by a foot, spun around and fell on his face in the dirt. We were all screaming as Tony strolled into the dugout like a hero. He was a hero at that point.

The seventh inning didn't start out the way we hoped. This big Polish kid on the mound was really bearing down in the clutch. He struck out our first batter Angelo Kenna on a blistering, 80 mph fastball. Then after Tag ran the count to three and two, Barnowski reached back and hurled a lightning bolt past poor Tag who just stood there stunned. Now everything fell back on Bobby, our star, our Babe Ruth, our home run hero to save the day and keep us in the game. The stands were alive with fans from Schenectady screaming at their kids to finish us off while our fans were scream- ing back with cheers for Bobby to knock it out of the park. After a brief conference on the mound between Barnowski and his man- ager, the battle between the two titans began.

Barnowski knew he couldn't be careless and send a fast ball down the middle of the strike zone or Bobby would crush it out of the park. So instead, he tried nibbling on the corners. He suck- ered Bobby into chasing a curve ball out of the strike zone that he dribbled foul past third base. Next he threw one inside that Bobby had to jump out of the way of.

"Ball one!" the umpire yelled, emphatically as the crowd oohed. Next he threw a blistering fastball at the knees that Bobby let go.

"Strike two," the ump yelled as he pivoted and pointed with vigor toward home plate.

The tension was incredible in the dugout and the stands. We are all praying that Bobby would pull it out and save the day, while the kids in the other dugout were praying that Barnowski would strike him out. It would become an incredible battle to the end. Bobby fouled off the next pitch, a curve ball. But then Barnowski started losing control. He threw a wild-pitch that went all the way back to the screen. He was lucky we had no one on base.

Now the count was two and two: a hitter's pitch for sure. Barnowski knew he had to get it over the plate or it would be a full count. Knowing Bobby would be looking for a strike, Barnowski whimped out and threw a soft curve ball way off the plate. That was when the Schenectady manager came out to talk to his ace and decided that it wasn't worth the chance: they would walk him intentionally now.

A dejected Bobby trotted down to first base knowing it was a blown opportunity. Now we were in a pickle. Coach had pulled Klasdi, our second best hitter, so Bobby could stay in the game. But now he had to find a pinch hitter to take his place. After discussing what to do with his assistant coaches, he came into the dugout and pointed to me again. "Ok, Herbie put your helmet on. You're pinch hitting.

"Oh my God", I thought to myself. "I got to face this freaking giant on the mound." Then I pondered why would coach pick me to make the final out, although I did have a great week of practice. I was either going to be a hero or goat if I struck out. If I struck out with the tieing run on base, I'd surely be the goat. I'd never live it down. My mind was racing. "How can I get out of this mess?" Then it came to me, I can weasel my way out by telling coach my finger still hurt. But then I realized I already told him it was ok when I was batting. I was screwed.

So there I stood in the batter's box, all five foot six inches of me looking at a ten foot ogre with steam spewing from his nostrils staring me down. It was frightening at first. But I braved it out. My knees were trembling as I scratched around in the batter's box waiting for the first lightning bolt to be launched in my direction. Within seconds it came like Zeus on the mountain top sending out a shard of golden light. Luckily it was about a foot over my head. "Ball one," the ump declared disappointedly as the crowd oohed.

I stepped out of the box and looked down at the coach hoping he might give me the bunt signal. I could handle getting thrown out trying to advance the runner or beating it out with my speed. But no such luck, I had to hit away. They were afraid Bobby might get thrown out at second because he wasn't too fast on his feet. I stepped back into the batter's box and twisted my feet around until I felt comfortable and within the blink of an eye the ball was in the catcher's glove. "Strike one," the rotund ump declared while hovering over me with his finger pointed at the plate.

"Geez," I said to myself. "I think this guy wants me out." So now I have the Schenectady crowd hissing at me, the ump hovering over me, and my teammates praying for me. With my head in a tizzy, I waited before stepping back into the box, closed my eyes and whispered a quiet prayer that I wouldn't embarrass myself to end this stupid game. After a few more seconds I stepped back into the box and took a deep breath. I looked the Devil, Barnowski in the eyes. They looked reddish green to me as little horns popped out of the corners of his cap. All of a sudden a serene peace came over me as the Devil took his long, slow windup. Then it happened, the 80 mph fastball floated toward me. It looked as big as a basketball as I swung my bat. Crrrrack!! The ball soared like a rocket toward center field. I could hear my teammates screaming in the background as this rocket took flight. It was like a missile rising, destined for its target—the center field scoreboard. I raced toward first base, euphoric; I was going to be a hero. Our fans were cheering as silence hovered over the Schenectady fans.

"Thud!" In a split second the cheers changed directions. Screams of joy from the Schenectady side and moans of grief from ours. My home run miracle became the miracle catch by their center fielder. His leap to glory turned my near home run into the agony of defeat for us.

I thought I was going to be treated like the goat that lost the game—I wasn't. My teammates all patted me on the back for my great effort and the coach came over, put his arm around my shoulder and told me I did a great job. "Herbie, you almost did it for us, I'm proud of you."

We limped home disappointed and sad, but as luck would have it Schenectady faltered in regional play and we got a chance to play them again at Hawkins Stadium in Menands. I got my first start playing center field, walked once, grounded out once, beat out an infield hit, and stole two bases. We won that game and went on to win several more in a round robin tournament, including beating Cohoes at their Intermediate field. I had two doubles that game, hitting the center field fence twice.

CHAPTER THIRTEEN

Sonny's Wedding and My First Official Kiss

A long with all the newness and excitement of being a freshman in high school, another huge family event took place that fall: my brother Sonny's wedding. Ma and my sisters talked about it incessantly during the summer and fall leading up to the wedding. It would be the first, big church wedding we ever had in our family. Most of our weddings were small events, with the receptions held in someone's house—Jack's was in Grandpa Davenport's house and Patty's in ours.

Sonny's fiancée Marge was a pretty, Irish Catholic girl from Watervliet. The wedding would take place in the late October at a huge brownstone church located on 19th Street in Watervliet. The reception would be held in Lansingburg at the Sunset Inn, an iconic banquet hall known for the classy events they hosted over the years. Thank goodness Marge's family had to pay for the reception because Ma and my sisters struggled to find just enough money to put their party dresses on layaway and hoped they would be paid off in time.

It would be the first time in my life that I would wear a suit. That spring, my brother Sonny, who was now a fireman, apparently didn't want me to look like an urchin at the wedding, so he brought me to Fitwell Clothiers next to the Hendrick Hudson Hotel to be fitted for a suit. I would have the suit for both Easter and his wedding. When he came back from the service and found a job, he bought all his clothes there. No more Stanley's or Grants for him. It seems he definitely wanted to remove the memories of being poor as soon as he could. I can't say as I blame him because he worked hard and earned that right.

He knew George, the store's tailor, very well. Along with buying his clothes there, Sonny would occasionally have a few beers at Callahan's restaurant on Fourth Street with George. Because of their friendly relationship, he was able to work out a deal to buy me a suit at a reduced price. Of course, buying an over-priced tuxedo for his wedding there didn't hurt either.

I was excited and thrilled that Sonny would do that for me because I rarely got anything new, although Ma and Dorothy had arranged for me to have new school clothes at the start of my freshman year. It felt weird standing in front of the huge, floor-to-ceiling mirror while George marked lines on the grayish brown trousers with white chalk. He also took the tape measure from around his neck and measured the inseam of my trousers, almost whacking me in the nuts. That felt really weird. He then told me to stand up straight so he could pin up the cuffs which were dragging on the floor. When he finished doing the same with my suit jacket, he told Sonny my suit would be ready next Friday. When we returned that day, I was amazed how well my new suit fit. All the excess material that had been hanging off me was removed. Now it fit like a glove. I guess 'Fitwell' was a good name for that shop.

On a brilliant fall day our whole family entered the church together, except my younger sisters who were not yet teenagers. They stayed home. I guess the cut-off criteria was that you had to be a teenager to attend. Poor Brenda, who really wanted to go to the wedding, had to stay home and watch my younger sisters Jan and Bonnie and my nephew Butch. Sadly, my father and Sonny had been estranged for whatever reason and Dad was nowhere to be found when we entered the church. He had long since moved out of the house and we had little contact with him.

I was fidgeting in my aisle seat next to Patty as the ceremony began, and for some unknown reason I glanced toward the back of the church. Maybe it was boredom or maybe it was the cool breeze filtering in through the open doors or maybe it was something else. Maybe God was giving me a signal to look since we were in church. Minutes earlier Marge had gone down the aisle in her elegant taffeta and silk gown, a radiant bride indeed. However, I had become mesmerized with the balding man who appeared at the top of the church stairs. Within seconds this short, stout man became silhouetted against the brilliant sunlight which made it appear he was in one of those stain glass windows depicting saints or angels with halos surrounding them. For sure, this couldn't have been my father, because everyone in my family considered him the farthest thing from an angel or saint.

Patty poked me in the ribs and I quickly returned my attention to the ceremony. I was wondering who this man could be, and why the hell Patty poked me. The ceremony seem to go on forever: vows were exchanged, prayers were offered, sparkling rings were placed on each other's hand. Finally, the priest pronounced them man and wife and Sonny kissed his bride.

When the organ rang out the iconic sounds of "Here Comes the Bride," I quickly turned around and realized the man standing stoically and proudly peering through the open door was my father. Although he wasn't invited to the wedding, he did manage to see Sonny get married. I was the only one who saw my dad standing there and I'm glad he saw his second son get married. (Years later I wondered if he was standing at the back of the church during my wedding, because everyone involved in my wedding insisted he not be invited. In hind sight, I should have insisted he be invited, but I didn't and I regret that. After all he was still my Dad.)

As Sonny and Marge were driven around in their limo and visited various areas of the city, we waited patiently for the doors to open at the banquet hall. My stomach was growling because I only had a bowl of soggy oatmeal for breakfast six hours earlier and I was a growing boy. Once inside we had to wait again in the cocktail lounge where people stood drinking and nibbling on hors d'oeuvres: finger sandwiches, various cheese and crackers, shrimp with cocktail sauce and Swedish meatballs. These were foods I never had before. I did have cheese and crackers before, but they usually were wrapped in cellophane and purchased at Harry Moore's store. I scarfed down as many meatballs as I could in as short a period as possible. Shrimp on the other hand? I wouldn't acquire a taste for that until I was a bit older. This day it smelled like cat food... Yuk!

After about an hour the cocktail party slowed as people appeared to get a bit agitated waiting for the bride and groom to arrive. "What's taking them so long?" Patty complained.

"They're touring Marge's neighborhood, Patty, so stop complaining," warned Ma.

"Why are they doing that? I'm starving," Patty whined.

"It's a tradition for the bride to show off to her neighbors who weren't invited."

"Well, that's a pretty stupid tradition."

"Be quiet. They're coming in now, shush!" Ma whispered.

Soon the side door of the restaurant opened and the wedding party entered in all their regalia as cheers erupted from the crowd in the bar. At that time, it was customary for the bride and groom to greet each guest at the door to the dining room. Sonny shook hands, smiled and laughed with the guys and hugged and kissed the ladies, while Marge for her part did the same.

However, being young, naïve and only a teenager, I didn't know about of this tradition. "Oh my God," I thought. "I'm going to have to kiss Marge." I was shocked and kind of excited at the same time. I had never kissed a woman before. The only experience I had kissing was when my sister Patty and Mickey Brighten had forced me and Butchie Grillo to play spin the bottle with Ellenor Kiljoy and Dena Wagener and when I kissed my sister Brenda when we were little kids around eight or nine. I remembered how yucky that was for us as little boys. Kissing girls, yuk! I think we would have rather kissed a frog than a girl at that age.

Finally, it was my turn to greet the bride. "Hi, Herbie," a radiant and smiling Marge greeted me. She held my hand and leaned toward me and before I knew it my lips were kissing the first woman I ever kissed in my life. I pulled away quickly and wondered what that waxy taste was. Befuddled over what just happened, I wiped my lips across the top of my hand and felt a gooey substance. I looked down and discovered a pinkish smudge on my hand. "So that's what lipstick tastes like, Yuk." I thought. I guess it was going to take me awhile to get used to that.

TROY BOYS CLUB DINNER—Youngsters at the Troy Boys Club who have excelled in activities at the club were honored at a dinner last night. Left to right are Leon Simon, Stanley Newman, Edward F. Ryan, the principal speaker; Herb Hyde, receiving an award as winner of the recent Junior Olympics competition, and Dom Geracitano, program director at the club.

JUNIOR OLYMPICS—The program of youth activities planned at the Troy Boys Club in observance of National Brotherhood Week started this week with a "Junior Olympics" competition. Here is Herbie Hyde chinning himself on the horizontal bar as Ted Potema scores the number of pull-ups.

CHAPTER FOURTEEN

Pudding Ego Before Brains

My basketball ego got me into trouble a couple times during freshman year. I was the leading scorer for the first five games or so, averaging eight points a game. My freshman coach Mr. Devito, for whatever reason, decided to start some different kids for a couple games. No longer being a starter, even though I was the team's leading scorer, really upset me. I soon began to whine to the other bench warmers and stupidly mouthed off to the coach about not starting. As a result, he suspended me a couple games for being disrespectful. Even though my shoe size was now a nine regular, I was still able to shove my foot in my mouth, earning my suspension.

After sitting out those games, I carefully watched what I said because I now knew the consequences. When I came back from my suspension, I had my best game ever against Catholic High, scoring nineteen points and running out the clock while being double teamed. We won that game by one point. That was the pinnacle of my high school sports career up to that point.

In addition to playing freshman basketball, I continued to play against kids from LaSalle and Catholic High at the Boys Club on Saturdays. Bobby Mahoney, who went to LaSalle and was a good four inches taller and forty pounds heavier than me, started pushing me around under the basket one Saturday. But that wasn't the worst part. The worst part was when he pushed me, slapped my hands and then laughed at me. I hated being laughed at. He must have thought that because I was small, I'd just take his crap. Wrong!

Finally, I had enough and shouted, "Stop pushing me around or I'm going to smack you, asshole." He just laughed harder and pushed me again. That's when I finally blew. I turned around, whacked him on the jaw and put him in the hospital. However, when I regained consciousness, I realized it wasn't exactly my powerful punch that sent him to the hospital. My teammates later told me that after I whacked him, he whacked me back. Apparently, my front teeth had taken a huge chunk out of his hand, requiring a trip to the hospital and several stitches. My teeth were loose for almost a month after that incident. During that period I became very fond of soup, Jello and pudding. It was touch-and-go for a while, but, luckily I didn't lose any teeth. Even though Bobby whacked me pretty good that day, he had a new found respect for me because I fought back.

The Boys Club had many good athletes who went on to very successful high school and college sports careers: Luther Rackley, Larry Sheffield, Billy Williams, and Leon Simon to name a few. I would never be as good as they were in basketball. However, as good as they were, I won the National Junior Olympics competition at the Club during my freshman year. (Being an old fart now as I write this, I wish I stayed as fit and thin as I was then.)

One of the finest athletes to ever come out of the Boys Club was a fellow named Billy Harrell. Although he had an opportunity to play basketball with the Harlem Globe Trotters, he turned it down to play his first love, professional baseball with the Cleveland Indians. A member of the Siena College Athletic Hall of Fame, he recently had his number retired during a touching, half time ceremony at the Times Union Center in Albany.

CHAPTER FIFTEEN

Broadway Abe

Troy, like so many other small towns and cities, had its share of memorable characters. Characters who touched people's lives in some manner. Be it tragic or funny, there was always something about them that stood out your mind. Someone you'd remember twenty, thirty or even fifty years later, in my case. One of the most memorable characters to me as a youth was a fellow called Broadway Abe. I believe he may have been a type-setter or copy boy at the Troy Record on Broadway.

Along with playing sports at school, I also began hanging out downtown with my school buddies. I had developed a love, or maybe it was hate, of playing pool. That love-hate relationship was probably caused in part by going to the Troy Boys Club all those years or being beaten in so many games of eight ball or rack by my friend Larry or other guys who'd hustle me out of what little money I had—especially when I was ahead and expected to win. I could be one sore loser and always took each loss personally. In my mind I rationalized that I didn't suck at pool but rather they cheated or were just plain lucky.

In any event, as I entered my teen years I'd go to a local pool hall called Whitey's. It was located on the third floor of the Market building, a triangular shaped building similar in style to the historic Flatiron Building in New York City. Situated on the northern tip of River and Third Streets and at the City's busiest intersection, Whitey's pool hall was a local hangout for both high school kids as well as local pool sharks. To get up to Whitey's you had to climb two flights of rickety, wooden stairs. At the top of the stairs was a huge, open room surrounded by windows, mostly on the west and north sides of the building. That room housed a dozen or so pool and billiards tables, as well as restrooms and a free standing, wooden telephone booth located next to the desk where you paid your hourly fee. In order to play and pay there was a punch clock, similar to what the many working class people would use to punch into work at places like Tiny Town Togs, Cluett and Peabody or Ford Motor Company in Green Island. That was how Whitey kept track of your playing time, with his punch clock.

Abe was a constant presence at Whitey's and would spend most afternoons socializing there after work. I had only seen Abe a few times but quickly realized that he was a huge Brooklyn Dodgers fan like me. However, what I didn't know about Abe was that being a Dodger's fan made him a Yankee hater. I guess it's normal for some sports junkies to hate their opponents.

One day after school, I decided I'd go to Whitey's before heading home. When I opened the door, I was greeted with thunderous sounds of what seemed to be a major fight going on upstairs. "You no good sons-a-bitches" screeched someone at the top of their lungs. That tirade was soon followed by what sounded like a pool stick being smashed against the front desk. "You fucking bastards," yelled Abe. Bam! It sounded like wood being smashed against wood.

"Stop it, you old coot," Whitey the owner yelled.

That was followed by streams of laughter cascading down the stairs as other guys yelled at the top of their lungs and banged their pools sticks on the floor. "Get em, Abe! Go get em." Stunned by the sound of this ruckus and with an adrenaline rush, I raced up the stairs hoping to get in on this fight. Out of breath and with my heart pounding, I fully expected to see bloodied bodies lying across pool tables. Instead, I was stunned to silence, watching as poor old Abe descended further into the depths of his rage. Although it sounded like a gang war, it was just Abe screaming at the top of his lungs into the telephone booth—using every expletive known to man—then slamming the door as hard as he could, because his beloved Dodgers had just been beaten again by the dreaded Yankees. Abe had listened to the end of the horrid game on the radio next to the telephone booth, and just like he had done on so many other occasions, he went off the deep end— much to the delight of the regulars who'd seen his antics in the past and always cheered him on.

"Don't egg him on, you assholes," Whitey yelled, pointing at Charlie Coots, Carl Redmond, Rabbit Riley, and Bugsy Mumfry. He feared Abe might have a heart attack during one of his tirades. Luckily, he never did.

I soon became accustomed to most of the harmless heckling that went on at Whitey's, but never became a hustler like some of my buddies did. In fact, Charlie Coots became quite a prolific pool player, competing with the likes of Rabbit Riley and Bugsy Murphy as well as Butch Leonard, who played at both Whitey's and Joe Canton's Pool Hall on Fourth Street. Butch was considered one of the best pool players ever to come out of Troy along with Joe Canton, himself.

CHAPTER SIXTEEN

High School/PTU /Service/Jail

Charlie, Billy Finch, Carl Redman and several other guys I hung around with when I was younger never finished school. They ended up in part-time school, AKA Part-Time-University or PTU, along with my brother Cliff. Most of them went into the service at some point in their late teens or early twenties. Some of the guys like Carl Redmond got their high school diplomas or GEDs in the service, while others like Alan, Denny, and I graduated from high school. Denny went to work after high school and Alan joined the service. Cliff ended up going into the service too, semi-voluntarily.

Unfortunately, Cliff began hanging out with a guy he had met in part-time school by the name of Johnny Horgan. One day Johnny decided to heist a car and take it for a joy ride. He saw Cliff hanging out by the Ahearn apartments and conned him into going along for the ride. However, the car's owner had called the cops. After gallivanting around town with Cliff riding shotgun for a couple hours, they both got arrested when they pulled up next to the Famous Lunch to get some hotdogs.

Two of Troy's finest, playing good cop/bad cop, conned Johnny into turning state's evidence and ratting on Cliff. They got him to claim that Cliff heisted they car even though he didn't. I guess they might have been out to get my brother because they knew his reputation as a troublesome tough guy. Johnny got off with a light sentence, probation, while Cliff ended up in the county lock-up because he wouldn't rat on Johnny. While in jail, Cliff got beat up by several inmates who tried to molest him, unsuccessfully. However, he got his face busted up pretty bad and had most of his front teeth knocked out. The jail report stated that he was injured playing leapfrog with other inmates. Supposedly, he accidentally hit his face on the bars and was sent to the emergency room at Samaritan Hospital to get checked out.

Ma didn't have the money to bail Cliff out, so he spent several weeks in the county jail until Tony Fermetti helped her get a bail bond. When he finally went back to court, the judge suspended the rest of his sentence, with the stipulation that he enter the military. But a week or two before he was supposed to leave for basic training, he had an interesting encounter with that louse, Johnny Horgan. Cliff, Alan and I were bullshitting with Ronnie Moore outside his store when Cliff spotted Johnny coming down College Avenue. "You son of a bitch," Cliff screamed at Johnny who turned around with a terrified look on his face. "I'm going to kill you!" Cliff picked up a red murphy and heaved it at Johnny who raced through the vacant lot at the back of the old Bassett building, just missing him, even though Johnny was a half a block away. Johnny never looked back but just kept running, never to be seen again. Ronnie and Alan restrained Cliff from running after him so he wouldn't get himself in any more trouble.

Cliff completed basic training and spent about a year on active duty. Even in the military, he managed to get in a bit of trouble. He joked when he was home on leave one time that he was training to drive a tank and accidently ran it over a nearby car, totally destroying the car. I'm not sure if that was true, but he was laughing his ass off telling his buddies about it down by Billy Bryce's house. When he finished his military duties, he worked several decent jobs which he'd end up losing for one reason or the other. He worked for a while with Dorothy and Jimmy at Tiny Town Togs. He then got a good job at the Bendix brake plant in Green Island, where he would eventually get laid off and never rehired.

His life was beginning to mirror Dad's in some ways. However, unlike Dad, Cliff eventually turned things around and had a productive life. He got a job working at Star Textile in Cohoes with the help of my brother-in-law, Steve Zayacheck. When the company moved its operations to Fuller Road in Albany, Cliff went with them and retired from there.

CHAPTER SEVENTEEN

Tiny Tim

Luckily, I had a growth spurt and by sophomore year I was 5' 9" and weighed 138 pounds. During that year I was moved to fullback on the JV team and also played linebacker on both the JV and varsity teams. Ronnie, Rocky Steward, Billy Conyers and Lee Bennett were also on that team. We didn't have a lot of size on our line that year, so one of the part time coaches, Jiggers Mallett, decided to invite a huge kid from his English class to try out for the team. His nickname was Tiny Tim Gushelman. He stood about 6' 2" and weighed about 350 pounds, huge but nimble. I was amazed during warm ups how easily he could touch his toes, even with his fifty-inch waist, while I, with my twenty-nine inch waist, could barely touch mine.

We had been practicing about a week when Tim arrived. Unfortunately, there weren't many practice uniforms that came close to fitting him. His upper body was so huge that his shoulder pads barely covered half the width of his shoulders. His head was so large and round that his leather helmet barely reached below his ears and looked like a giant peanut resting on top of his head. Looking at him in awe and disbelief, I noticed something strange about his body. Although he had a massive upper torso and humongous gut, his legs didn't look big enough to carry that mammoth load. But that didn't deter him or the coach. He willingly ran laps, did all the calisthenics, and seemed primed to give football his best shot. The field was muddy and slippery from about an inch of rain we had earlier that week. We all struggled to push the blocking sled around in the slop, while Coach Mallett, who had perched himself on top of the sled for added weight, screamed at us to push harder. We continued our individual struggles to push the sled as far as we could, but that didn't satisfy coach. Apparently disgusted with our meager efforts, coach decided to embarrass us by using someone else as a positive example of how it should be done. So he enlisted his prime, shiny, new recruit Tiny Tim to set that example. "Ok, you clowns," Coach Mallett whistled, through the gap in his front teeth. "This is how it's done. Get over here Tiny and show them how to do it the right way," pointing at the rusty, mud-covered sled.

Tiny was now huffing and puffing and sweating like a pig as he stationed himself in back of the sled awaiting coach's instructions. Hearing the commotion while working with the running backs on the other side of the field, Coach Del Vecchio wandered over to see what was going on. He stood on the sidelines amused as Tiny got down into a three-point stance. "Ok, at the count of three I want you to push that sled to the twenty-five yard line without stopping. Do you hear me, Tiny?"

"Yes, sir." Tiny huffed.

"Ok," said Coach Mallett, standing in back of Tiny with a football in his hands and squatting as though he was taking a snap. "Ready, set: hut...hut, hut." On the last hut, Tiny lunged forward as hard as he could in hopes of moving the sled like the coach expected him to do. But instead of moving the sled and showing us all up, Tiny got stuck. His hulking body was tightly wedged against the sled, and his feet were sunken about a foot into the mud. He was unable to move the sled or himself an inch.

It took four linemen to pry the sled away from Tiny, causing him to fall face first into the slop. They then had to lift Tiny's muddy body out of the muck and onto a wooden bench. Half the team tried to stifle their laughter, while Coach Mallett glared at them in disgust and told them to shut up. Poor Tiny sat on the bench as the coaches huddled to determine his fate. Some of the older guys went over to console Tiny while others snickered behind his back. The end result of this debacle: Tiny went back to playing tuba in the marching band.

CHAPTER EIGHTEEN

I Get the 'Kurse'

Most junior varsity players got to play in some of the varsity games when the score was lop-sided (usually we were on the losing end of those lop-sided scores) or when somebody got hurt. We weren't very good back then. (Today Troy High has a power-house football program.) However, we JV players did play quite a bit in our game against our arch rival, Catholic High. We beat them by a score of twenty-six to twelve. A local sports writer, Perry Wood, affectionately nicknamed us subs "The Rinky Dinks" for our stellar play. We actually scored a touchdown that game along with first string fullback Freddie (Ace) Case who lumbered his way to an ungainly, sixty-yard touchdown. I think that one touchdown was the offensive highlight of his career.

During my second JV game I was injured when six Linton *goons* wearing football helmets piled on top of me after an eight-yard run. They kicked me in the teeth, chipping one of those hard little nobs off my front tooth, and had to be pulled off me by the refs and my teammates. I could barely breathe until the pile was finally un-tangled. Even then, the coach refused to let me play the rest of the game because I was having so much trouble breathing.

That night, a worried Ma sent me to get checked out by Dr. Kowlenger. He said my ribs were probably not broken, just severely bruised. Whether bruised or broken, the protocol is the same: tape them up. He said it would take about three weeks to heal enough to go back and play, which didn't sit well with our new volunteer assistant coach, Mr. Kurse. He would come to be my nemesis later on. He called me a baby for wearing a flack-jacket to protect my ribs when I returned to practice two weeks later.

The Saturday following my injury, my sister Brenda introduced me to her friend Joanne Hager during the varsity game against Linton. She lived in Albia, and, after the game, I offered to walk her home because she had just missed the three o'clock bus, and it would be an hour before the next one. She seemed really friendly, so we agreed to meet at the dance that night. She treated me like a wounded warrior. Boy, did that make me feel important. Nothing like being an injured jock to steal the hearts of the ladies.

Because I was still in a lot of pain, I wasn't able to jitterbug with Brenda or Joanne. I just sat in the bleachers and watched them tear up the floor, jitterbugging and doing the stroll and all. But, luckily, Joanne asked me to dance the last dance, a slow Elvis tune, "Love me Tender." She took my hand as we walked out to the middle of the floor. It almost felt like my last dance with Lois during grade school, when she put her head on my shoulder. But it was not exactly the same. I could feel myself stirring, emotionally and physically, because we were so close. The scent of her hair and the warmth of her body were bringing me to a place where I began to feel uncomfortable and not in control. Luckily, the dance was a short one, otherwise an unforeseen crisis may have popped up.

Joanne eventually ended up dating another guy in her class even though we talked several times on the telephone, and it appeared we might become good friends. As usual, things didn't work out for me with a girl. I remember how annoying I was at the time and regret being such a jerk on the phone when she asked me to go on a hayride. I thought at the time that hay rides were lame, even though I had never been on one.

Coach Kurse and I had a rocky relationship throughout my sports career in high school. Not only had he become a volunteer assistant coach in football; he was also the junior varsity basketball coach. I did make the JV team, although as a reserve, even though I arrogantly thought I should have been a starter. Coach Kurse turned out to be even meaner and nastier as our basketball coach than he was as our assistant football coach. I think he was still reliving his college glory days and apparently never outgrew them. On his office wall he posted an article from the 1950's with a photo of himself making "The shot heard around the world." From beyond half court, he had made the winning shot in a Catholic basketball tournament at Madison Square garden—a pretty impressive feat. However, it seemed to many of us aspiring basketball players that his ego was bigger than he was. In fact, while sitting on the bench waiting to get our chance to play, we'd joke about him sitting in his office with his feet up, smoking a cigar and admiring that article endlessly.

My biggest thrill after making the junior varsity team was getting get a brand new pair of sneakers. Now I wouldn't have to wear those beat up, black Keds anymore. Back in the early sixties, it was "shoe time" when the shoe salesman brought in boxes of brand new sneakers for everyone to try on. I can't remember the brand name, but I do know they weren't Nike's. Nike's weren't invented yet. As it turned out, getting those brand new sneakers would be the highlight of my JV career aside from a couple of interesting games I did get to play in. My sophomore experience playing basketball made me long for the glory days of my freshman year which was mostly a positive experience for me. As a freshman, I remember going to my first away game at Mount Pleasant. After we were soundly whooped, we showered and came back to the gym to hear their raucous crowd screaming. The thing I remember most about the varsity game was watching a little guy by the name of Joey Loudis diving for loose balls and passing off to a gigantic ogre named Ernie who would bully his way to the hoop for an easy lay-up. For years Mount Pleasant had solid sports programs in football, basketball and baseball, along with another Schenectady school called Nott Terrace, which later became Linton High School.

Troy High at that time, solid? Not so much. However, in the not too distant future (1964-1965), Troy High would reach its pinnacle for high school basketball. They were recognized by Adolph Rupp, legendary basketball coach for the University of Kentucky, and various media sports outlets around the country as the best high school basketball team in America. That undefeated Troy High team featured: Rosie Phillips, Luther Rackley, Steve and Jerry Guter, Bobby Wood, Perry Ashley, Hubert Terry and others and was coached by Clem Zotto.

Tony Yates, Timmy Maxwell and I sat on the bench ninety percent of most games. Being disgruntled bench warmers, we whispered and whined about not getting any playing time, even though our team was usually getting clobbered. That fact indicated to us that the starters weren't doing such a good job. However, the coach didn't seem fazed as he continued to keep his starters in. it seems the coach had his favorites and was reluctant to give anyone else a chance, especially me. I guess he had no confidence in our ability even though we worked hard in practice every day. I worked hard but struggled with stamina. You see, I still didn't know I was suffering from asthma. The coach never realized it either. He thought I was dogging it or faking it when I was bent over gasping for breath. Instead of asking me what the problem was, he would just yell at me then order me to the bench.

I remember in one home game we were getting clobbered in the first half—throwing passes away, taking stupid fouls and allowing easy lay-ups. At half-time we were sitting in the locker room as coach started his usual harangue of the starters and us subs. The team manager (ball boy) always had sliced oranges ready for all the players to suck on during half time, which gave them a little sugar high for the second half. However, coach was so upset with the starters that he wouldn't let us poor subs (who had nothing to do with the on-court debacle) have any orange slices, usually the only thing we looked forward to in most games. I guess he had to punish us for the starters' lousy play. Go figure.

For away-games, all the players received a small stipend, usually seventy-five cents, to buy some food after the game since we didn't have team meals. After a horrendous loss at Amsterdam one Friday night, coach was so upset that he didn't give us our stipend. That was a shock, especially to me because I was starving and looked forward to using my stipend on a half dozen hot dogs at the Famous Lunch. Instead, I went home hungry. To make matters worse, coach had us report that Saturday morning for an 8:30 am practice. When we got suited up in our practice duds, he had us run laps upstairs around the balcony for a half-hour, non-stop. When he finally came out of his office, he screamed at us to come downstairs, tossed a bag full of basketballs onto the court and told us to practice by ourselves. He then went back into his office not to be seen or heard again until 10:30 when he came out and told us to go home.

Now to one of those interesting games I *did* get to play in. During a Friday night game at Phillip Schuyler, I was doing my usual whining on the bench along with Tony and Timmy about not playing since we were getting clobbered again. Hearing us whining, coach leaned over and told us to shut up or we'd never get to play in a game. Soon after that little tete-a-tete, he pulled Steve Dawalski, who now had four fouls, out of the game. He put Tony in to replace Steve, all the while glaring at me and Timmy. Tony played the rest of the game, while Timmy and I sat at the far end of the bench steaming in silence. Steve, on the other hand, was mumbling and whining about being pulled from the game. Of course, coach never heard Stevie's whining. Apparently, he only had ears for *our* whining.

The next night we played Linton at home. This game was much closer than the twenty point loss we had suffered the night before. But unbelievably, we were only trailing by five points with about six seconds left on the clock when coach called time out after one of our players fumbled a pass out of bounds. Figuring we didn't have a chance to win, he arrogantly stormed down to the end of the bench with a sly grin on his puss. "Ok, Hydie, go in for

Dawalski. Since you're such a hot shot defensive player, I'm sure you'll steal the inbound pass." I'm sure he thought sending me in with so little time left would be the ultimate insult. Well, guess what? I checked in, stole the inbound pass and made a lay-up, bringing the crowd to its feet and bringing us within three points as the clock ran out. The crowd going wild when I made that layup surely pissed off coach to no end.

CHAPTER NINETEEN

Bucksters

As high school moved along, I began to recognize the haves and have not's. The haves, you know, the kids who were in the cliques, the upper echelon of school. I got along pretty well with most of them but didn't meet their social status requirements. Instead, I became part of my own little clique of misfits: Billy and Larry. We called ourselves the Unholy Three.

Although Ronnie was still a close friend, he was not a charter member of our little club. Ronnie and I had a separate set of friends because of sports. Ronnie was known as a very good hockey player outside of school and fit in better than me with the upper crust cliques because of his outgoing personality. However, I don't think that he socialized much with them either. (It was during this time when I was slowly gaining a sense of the social, cultural and economic strata of our country through the microcosm of high school.)

Unlike me, Billy and Larry didn't do sports in high school. Although I did, I was not real close with my sports buddies and teammates. We rarely interacted socially. Most jocks were in the upper echelon cliques, along with cheerleaders and social and student government leaders. Even though I did have one good friend who was a cheerleader, Terry Mahoney, we didn't hang out socially.

I drifted away from my sports buddies when I stopped participating during my junior year. I was cut from the varsity basketball team, in part because of a problem with my junior varsity coach Mr. Kurse who held a grudge, forever. When I got cut from the varsity team, he wouldn't let me play on the junior varsity—which had always been the practice in the past. The varsity coach said I could be the equipment manager if I wanted to. To me, that was an insult worse than getting cut. With my ego destroyed, I decided to give up competitive sports for good and began to concentrate on my other loves—art and music. However, I did continue to play intramural sports and drums in the concert and marching band as well as singing in the school chorus and glee club.

Although we were far from being nerds, Billy, Larry and I felt a little bit like reluctant outcasts. Billy and Larry especially disliked the upper crust cliques. They called the ones they disliked most *Bucksters*. It was a name Larry and Billy invented, along with a not-so-secret sign and ritual we performed when one was around. We held up the middle three fingers of our right hand then stamped our right foot three times as they walked by. We then laughed like hell as they wondered what we were doing. The definition of a Buckster: A three-fingered phony. I guess we were pretty presumptuous thinking others kids were phonies. Who knows, maybe the kids we pulled this stunt on thought we were phonies too, but they didn't have a cool signal to use like we did.

CHAPTER TWENTY

Wine, Wine, Water, Water—
Dispensation for Life.

I became semi-serious about religion starting around the age of ten when my sisters and I were baptized at Saint Paul's Episcopal Church in Troy. Grandma and Grandpa Davenport stood up for us as our God parents. I don't think too many people can remember when they were baptized. However, why we weren't baptized as infants remains a mystery to me. My sisters and I began attending religious instructions around age eight and went to church services with my sister Dorothy. As we got older, we went by ourselves. Midway through the ten o'clock mass on Sunday, parish kids were dismissed to attend church school at the parish guild house next door. We also were required to attend classes there after school on Wednesdays. We had to pass those classes in order to be confirmed later.

I really didn't like Sunday school classes. I would rather have stayed and sang hymns since I've always loved singing. Religious instructions: not so much. Confirmation was an important sacrament in the Episcopal tradition and I reluctantly studied in order to fulfill my commitment to my faith. Soon after confirmation, assistant Pastor Harmon took me aside and asked me to become an acolyte. He felt it would be a rewarding opportunity for me to grow in the church. I know Ma always respected both him and Reverend Platte. Both ministers had visited Ma on occasion to make sure things were all right in our household. You don't see that kind of personal outreach today, or maybe you do and I just don't see it.

I wasn't sure at first if I really wanted to make the kind of commitment needed, mainly because it would mean getting my lazy butt out of bed early each Sunday. But the selling point for me was that, once I gained seniority, I could earn a little money working weddings and funerals. I never quite gained the needed seniority—even after two years of service. It seemed like all the older acolytes got the gravy while I didn't even get the scraps. Being an acolyte offered me a unique opportunity to delve into the workings of the church. I was able to see how pastors worked and ministered to people inside and outside their parish. You may find this hard to believe, but at one point in my life I almost considered becoming a minister. However, with my many experiences and antics, I wonder how that would have worked out.

I was nervous the Saturday before I was to serve my first mass and didn't sleep well due to the anxiety I was feeling. I was worried that I would screw up and that I'd look like a fool in front of the whole congregation. "Herbie, wake up," Ma whispered.

"Uh, k, Ma," I mumbled before rolling over and immediately falling back into a deep sleep. Five minutes later Ma shook me and yelled.

"Herbie, get out of bed now! You're going to be late for your first service." She then pulled the blankets off me and stood there until I dragged my scrawny butt out of bed. "Get dressed, brush your teeth and comb your hair. You have to be presentable if you're going to be an acolyte."

"Ok, ok, Ma," I whined back, then slithered into the bathroom and got myself ready. I sat at the table and asked Ma what was for breakfast.

"Herbie, did you forget everything you learned in class already? You don't eat breakfast before communion, you have to fast."

"Holy crap" I thought to myself. "Boy, this really stinks," I grumbled, "I'm starving," not thinking Ma would hear me.

"Herbie, stop complaining. You can wait until you come home for breakfast. Fasting is part of your religion and you know it so stop your whining."

All the way down the hill to church I went over in my mind exactly what I was supposed to do during the service and began to feel a little more comfortable the closer I got. I opened the heavy oak door to the vestibule on the east side of this gothic, granite church and a sense of awe struck me. I was about to do something no one in my family had done before. As I opened my assigned locker (number five), I saw for the second time the cassock and surplice I would wear and that would mark me as a special individual.

Having just completed an intensive three-week boot camp on proper church etiquette, I felt a sense of pride in what I was about to do for the first time. I didn't want to mess it up because I knew Ma was so proud of me and didn't want to diminish that pride. As I was putting on my gear, I went over in my head: Wine, wine, water, water! That was the sequence I had to use when preparing the wine for communion.

I entered the sanctuary with my lit taper, lit all the proper candles, and didn't burn down the church. I was off to a good start. Then came the procession. Reverend Hellman and the assistant pastor Reverend Harman led us from the sacristy in slow methodical steps, while the organ played in the background. So far, so good. Then it was time to help prepare the wine and the host. First, I had to put a white linen napkin over my left wrist, like a waiter in a high class res-taurant. Next I had to take the tops off the Waterford crystal cruets, located on a sterling silver tray at the side of the altar. With the cruet containing the wine in my left hand and the one containing water in my right, I had to glance out into the congregation and count the first three rows of people, then multiply by four to get an estimate of how many people were there for the early morning communion. If I was off and Reverend Hellman had too many hosts, he had to eat the extras. Reverend Helllman hated extras! "Shit," I thought as I stood there counting in my mind, "how much is thirteen times four?"

"What's the count, what's the count?" Reverend Hellman sternly whispered.

"Uh, sixty-five I think." (I always sucked at math.)

"Are you sure?" Reverend Hellman glared down at me.

"Uh, Uh, I think so," I murmured back. It was then time to finish preparing the wine and host. As the Reverend held out his gold chalice, I cautiously poured a little wine—waited two seconds then poured a little more.

"Give me more than that young man!" Reverend Hellman de-manded, at which time my hands began to shake and I spilled some on his shoes and splashed some on the marble floor.

"Uh, oh," I thought. "I'm in trouble now." If looks could kill, I was dead and headed straight to hell before I finished my first communion service. It was then that the Reverend took the water cruet from my hand and finished preparing the wine himself.

I anxiously sat in a chair by the side of the altar as Reverend Hellman and Reverend Harmon continued with the service: The Sermon, the offering, the Lord's Prayer and the Lamb of God taking away the sins of the world. I worried the Lamb of God wouldn't take away the ones I just committed. As part of the service, I had to kneel at the brass rail that separated the congregation from the altar. Just as Reverend Hellman approached me with the host, I started getting sick to my stomach and dizzy. Snap! I heard a sound in my subconscious state then a burning sensation in my nose as the smelling salts Reverend Harmon placed under my nose brought me back to the conscious world. Still groggy, I cautiously accepted the host from Reverend Hellman and was then assisted to my chair by Reverend Harmon—where I finished the service.

Immediately after the service my inquisition began. "I had to eat over twenty extra wafers because you didn't count right," complained Reverend Hellman.

"I'm sorry, Reverend, I must have miscounted. I won't do it again."

"You better not, young man."

"Yes, Sir," I replied.

"Now, young man, we have the matter of you passing out."

"I'm sorry, Reverend Hellman. I don't know what happened to me."

"Did you eat breakfast this morning, Herbie?" Reverend Harmon asked with a slightly more sympathetic tone in his voice.

"No, Sir. Ma reminded me I had to fast before communion." That was when both pastors huddled in the corner discussing my situation. After a couple minutes, Reverend Harmon returned, as Reverend Hellman left the sacristy with a scowl on his face. I wondered how he could smile and be friendly to his congregation as they left church but never seemed to be able to offer a smile for me.

"Well, Herbie, that was quite a start for you today," Reverend Harmon chuckled. "But we will work on it. You will get better, I promise. We just discussed the reason why you fainted this morning and Reverend Hellman agreed, reluctantly, that you have to eat breakfast before you attend mass from now on. We can't have you fainting on the altar any more. So we are officially giving you a dispensation. I will write a note for you to take home to your mom so she will understand. However, I want you to come here Wednesday after school so we can practice some of the things you had problems with today. I have a lot of faith in you, Herbie, and I'm willing to take the chance that you will succeed. Are you willing to work with me on this, Herbie?"

"Yes, Sir, I am," I meekly replied. As time passed I *did* get better. In fact, I actually became quite good at it. However, in the two and a half years I remained an acolyte, Reverend Hellman never recommended me once to work a wedding or funeral. Acolytes who worked those services received a little money from the families as part of their gift to the church for performing the service.

Ironically, this was around the same time I worked caddying for Reverend Hellman at the exclusive Troy Country Club. I vividly remember dodging fifty golf balls I shagged for him, lugging his expensive golf clubs for eighteen treacherous holes with hills that even Billy-goats couldn't climb, and listening to him yell at me for minor mistakes. To add insult to injury, he gave me a measly quarter for two and a half hours of hard work. It was then I decided to give up being both an acolyte and caddy.

I became disillusioned because I felt the Reverend had no respect for me as a person. Sure, I had made mistakes, I was still a kid, and kids make mistakes. His haranguing made me feel inferior. I lost some respect for him because what he did was contrary to how I felt spiritual leaders should act toward ordinary people. I now thought of him as elite, materialistic and unfeeling. However, I still respected Reverend Harmon. He was leaving to go to his new parish in Waterford; although I liked Reverend Pratt, his replacement, I didn't know him that well. So, although I still went to church regularly after resigning, I was able to sleep in on Sunday mornings and attend the later mass. Plus, I kept my dispensation because they never rescinded it, thank God.

CHAPTER TWENTY ONE

VD and Me?

Teenagers, especially teenage boys, begin to experience self-gratification as soon as they begin sprouting pubic and facial hair, while other kids start much earlier. I can attest to that. (Grade school boners and how to hide them come to mind.) However, when I started to "find religion", I began to have mixed emotions about indulging in those manual escapades. I became torn between protestant guilt and exquisite pleasure. Most times the latter won out. I was so naïve about sex as a young teen. Today's teenager would think I was an idiot with my thoughts about those things. My classmates reading this today will probably think I was an idiot too. But I actually believed some of the stuff I heard about bathroom diseases. It stuck like glue in my brain, the same way taffy stuck to my teeth.

Not having my older brothers around to teach me the true facts about these things plus not taking health courses in high school left me vulnerable to this massive misinformation. I had listened to all those old wives tales about catching diseases from dirty toilet seats. Guys would talk about getting crabs or the clap from all kinds of sources. But hearing how filthy and scary public toilet seats were from my older sisters made a lasting impression on me and I always tried to avoid using them. These silly, irrational thoughts affected my life in a way I'm almost embarrassed to talk about. But I will anyway. At one time, I actually believed I had contracted a disease from sitting on a filthy toilet seat at the old State Theater.

I had a stomach bug and severe cramps the Saturday I went to the theater. I tried to hold back from going to the men's room but couldn't. So I reluctantly entered the dilapidated stall and immediately I felt a wave of nausea. I held my breath, quickly yanked down my jeans, and then plopped my scrawny butt on the filthiest toilet I'd ever seen. I made it just in time, as the steaming effluent gushed out, splattering the bowl and making the room smell even worse. But that wasn't the worst part. When I flushed the toilet, my private parts got sprayed with all kinds of germy gunk, but I couldn't clean myself right away because another guy had just entered the room. He was gagging from the smell as he used the urinal next to my stall. After he left, I tried to clean myself at the sink but had to rush, fearing another guy might come in and see me before I finished. He might have thought I was some kind of pervert or, worse yet, maybe *he* was a pervert. The thought that I had exposed myself to all those germs played in the back of my mind, muted, but always there. Had I picked up the clap, syphilis or the crabs? The thought haunted me for months.

During this same time period I developed a weird habit. Sometimes when I got up in the morning, my pubic area felt itchy. Could it be a bad case of pubic dandruff or something more onerous? Sometimes when on the toilet, I would sit and daydream while waiting for nature to take its course during my daily ritual. However, I would also twirl a single strand of pubic hair in an effort to satisfy this annoying itch and, if that didn't satisfy it, I painfully yanked it out at the roots. After doing that I noticed a slimy substance at the base of the hair and warily wondered what the hell that crap was. Yanking out that hair seemed to satisfy the itch temporarily. This annoying habit then spread to my head like a virulent disease overtaking my body and psyche.

Then my problems really started. I was watching a documentary about Al Capone one night while twirling strands of hair near my cowlick—yanking out the most annoying ones to assuage my imaginary itching problem. After glancing at the slimy ends, I tossed them away. I heard how Al Capone had died of syphilis, a horrid venereal disease that my sisters called a "bathroom disease." The narrator described the horrors of the disease and its many symptoms, one of which was losing your hair.

It was that moment when my sister Brenda came into the room and yelled to Ma: "Hey Ma, I think Herbie's going bald!" She then began laughing out loud, "You're going bald, Herbie."

"No, I'm not!" I screamed back at her.

"Stop it, you two," Ma said as she walked into the parlor, a cup of coffee in her hand. It was then that she saw me twirling my hair again. She had warned me about doing that a week before, but I was unable to stop the nasty habit. "How many times do I have to tell you, Herbie? Stop pulling your hair! " She then walked over to where I was sitting Indian-style on the floor and brusquely pulled my hand away. "Damn it, you *are* losing your hair. Stop it now or you will be completely bald before you know it!"

That was the statement that sent shock waves rushing like a hurricane across my mind. "Holy shit," I thought. "I am going bald, Al Capone went bald, so I must have syphilis!" My mind raced back to the bathroom incident at the State Theater and now I was in panic mode. What the hell was I going to do? How could I tell Ma? Was I going to die like Al Capone? What could I do? I was totally paranoid.

Next week was the start of my junior year, and football practice began a week later. But before I could play, I had to have a physical by the school physician, Doctor Pallavino. Ironically, I had a physical my freshman and sophomore year and vividly remembered how he checked my private parts for a hernia. So now I was scared to death to be examined, knowing he would check my private parts again and would find this horrible, venereal disease. I would be exposed to the whole world. How would I explain it to Ma? But even more ominously, I feared he would he tell me I was doomed to die a horrible death!

"Dear Lord, please forgive me for masturbating all those times," I prayed. I hoped that I would be saved by promising not to sin again. I would stop fantasizing about Annabell Smithers and Diane Howard my neighbors, as well as several members of our cheerleading team, Candy, Sherry and Karla with the big boobs.

Monday morning the parade to the school nurse's office started. I almost passed out from fear when the telephone rang. I knew it was the nurse's office calling for me or one of my teammates to come for their physical. Mrs. Rogers held the phone against her chest, looked up and down the aisle, stared at me and pointed. "Rocky Stewart, report to the nurse's office."

"Ok, Mrs. Rogers," Rocky happily shouted as he tapped me on the shoulder rushing by. Rocky was one of my buddies on the JV team and we both looked forward to playing first string varsity this year. He was a good looking jock, muscular and sporting a brush cut like many other jocks. I was getting more nauseated waiting for the axe to fall. The next call was for Dick O'Connell, then Ronnie, and the last that morning was for Lee Bennett. Phew, I dodged a bullet because the doctor only did physicals twice a week on Mondays and Thursdays, and he apparently met his quota for Monday before he reached me. But that didn't solve my problem, it just delayed it. What the hell was I going to do when I did get the call?

That afternoon, Coach Del Vecchio called a meeting for all potential players to discuss the upcoming season and how we could improve on our pathetic, one-and-seven season the year before. He also noted that this year, for the first time (to instill a sense of camaraderie) all varsity members could purchase team jackets for the unbelievable low price of twenty dollars from Cahill's Sporting Goods. The price may have been unbelievably low for some kids, but it was way too expensive for me. Ma didn't have that kind of extra money lying around.

"Man, that's sharp!" Rocky beamed as he tried on one of the samples coach had brought to the meeting.

"Make sure you sign up today with your jacket size and bring me a check by the end of next week so we can order them in time for the start of the season," Coach said. He then closed the meeting stating, "You should all have your physical done by this Thursday or you will be disqualified from playing this year. Do all of you understand?"

"Yes, sir!" we all shouted back in unison.

Needless to say, I had a couple sleepless nights worrying about what to do come Thursday. "Are you ok, Herbie?" Ma asked when she saw that I hadn't touched my breakfast.

"Uh, I'm ok, Ma. I'm just not hungry."

"Well, at least eat your toast and drink your juice or you'll get sick."

"Ok, Ma," I grudgingly agreed.

When I sat down at my desk at school I could feel my heart racing. I knew I would have to face the music soon but still didn't know what to do. Then it happened! I heard my teacher's staccato command, "Herbie, report to the nurse's office."

My heart sunk, my stomach churned and I almost threw up. It's happening. I can't escape anymore. I just sat there for a few moments, depressed, scared to death, unable to move.

"Herbert! Didn't you hear me?" Mrs. Rogers yelled down to me again.

I looked up and mumbled "Yes, Mrs. Rogers, I heard you." I then stood up and shuffled out to the hall and made up my mind. Instead of turning to go to the nurse's office I headed to the southern exit of the building, went down to the first floor and walked out of school. I quickly headed down the concrete steps before anyone saw me. The sun felt warm as I headed south on Burdett Avenue towards Tibbetts Ave, then east for a block, turned right and down the hill toward Brunswick Road. I was in a stupor, meandering aimlessly as cars whizzed by. I almost got hit by several as I walked against traffic with my head down. My mind was limp with depression about what to do. I had just created more problems because I left school without permission, and I still couldn't come to grips about how to deal with this horrible disease I'd imagined.

Before I knew it, I was standing on the entry road to the Troy Country Club, which brought back bad memories about my run in with Reverend Hellman. Ironically, he usually played golf on Thursday with several local doctors. (I guess Thursdays were doctors and wealthy pastors day to play golf.) That's when an idea popped into my mind. I would go to church and ask God to forgive my sins, knowing he would guide me through this nightmare and Reverend Hellman wouldn't be there to harangue me.

By the time I reached Saint Paul's, it was almost 12:30. No one was around as I sought refuge in the sanctuary, kneeling and praying frantically for God to answer my prayers and guide me. I must have said a half dozen Lord's Prayer's, plus a dozen Hail Mary's, even though I wasn't Catholic. Suddenly, calm came over me, as light streamed in from the sacristy. It must be God coming to rescue me, I thought. He would tell me what to do, he would save me. Within seconds a huge silhouette approached the altar with his arms spread wide, bowing in front of the cross, then turned to face me as an aura of light engulfed him.

"Oh, my God, it's God!" I thought. "He is going to save me."

Tears of relief began streaming down my cheeks as my depression lifted from my soul and comfort engulfed me under my now closed eyes.

"Is that you, Herbert?" an ominous voice called out. "What are you doing here? You should be in school!"

My eyes popped open.

"Oh shit," I thought. "It's not God. It's Reverend Hellman! He must not have played golf today." He started down from the altar heckling me about being out of school as I quickly got to my feet, bowed, then raced like hell out the door. The relief and euphoria I had begun to feel a few minutes earlier were gone. I felt like a dark shroud had been thrown over me. Depression, despair, fear and frustration seized me, as my mind struggled to find a way to deal with the worst emotional crisis I faced since the death of Grandpa Davenport.

Distraught, I headed toward the river, soon arriving at the base of the Congress Street Bridge. I walked north for a while, watching as seagulls swooped down and gathered their late afternoon lunch. How lucky they were. No worries, no cares cushioned by the warm, late summer breezes. How I yearned for those comforting childhood dreams. In them I was able to escape my worries, flap my arms and away I'd go, soaring over the city and feeling safe and free just like the seagulls.

I walked along Front Street until I reached the base of Fulton Street near the Hendrick Hudson Garage. As I approached the crumbling concrete sea wall, I noticed the stairway where I had fished for eels and bullheads with Alan many years earlier. Since we didn't have real fishing poles, we used a long stick cobbled together with twine and diaper pins I stole from Ma one day. I remembered, not so fondly, how bad the river smelled that day and the fact that we didn't catch anything but a couple of turds. The sun was beginning to slink behind the oil tanks that lined the river bank on the Watervliet side of the mighty Hudson. As I mulled over my future, sitting precariously on the edge of that decrepit concrete wall, I shivered from the late afternoon chill. No, I didn't have thoughts of jumping in. I had to get home before it got too late and face the music. If the school had contacted Ma, I would be in deep, deep trouble. But I realized I had to do it.

When I finally made it home and warily opened the front door, there stood Ma with her arms crossed, glaring at me. "Ok! Where were you all day?"

I looked down at my feet and sheepishly replied. "I, uh, didn't feel good and left school. I was afraid to go to the nurse because I thought she would send me home and I didn't want to ruin my Perfect Attendance," I lied. "I figured that if I got some fresh air I would feel better and could go to my next class after study hall and not miss anything." I continued to lie.

"Do you really expect me to believe that baloney, Herbie? The truant officer came to our house this morning looking for you. I couldn't believe it was you he was looking for and not your brother Cliff. (Cliff had dropped out of school several years earlier.)

"I won't do it again, Ma." I promised.

"Well, how can I believe you now, Herbie? You're lying through your teeth and you know it. What is going on? Do you know how much trouble you've caused? You could be suspended from school." It was then that I burst into tears, crying uncontrollably. Ma rushed over and hugged me as I almost collapsed from the stress. "What's the matter, Herbie? What is going on?" She was almost in tears herself trying to figure out what was happening to me. She sat me down next to her on the parlor couch, then shooed my nosey sisters into the kitchen so we could talk in peace.

"Something is wrong with me, Ma." I cried. "I can't tell you because it's too personal and I think I might die from it."

"Herbie, you have to tell me so I can help you!" Ma pleaded. "What is it, Herbie, what is it?"

"I can't tell you, Ma, I'm too ashamed."

Beside herself, Ma wasn't sure how to handle me in this condition. I was so distraught. Maybe when my brother Sonny came home from work, she would call him to take me to see Dr. Kowlenger, our family doctor, and have me checked out. Besides I would probably need a doctor's note in order to get back to school without being suspended. "It can't be as bad as you think, Herbie," Ma soothed. "Dr. Knowlenger is a good doctor and I'm sure he will be able to treat you if there is anything serious going on. Ok, Herbie? Ok?"

Feeling her soothing words and her loving arms around me helped me to relax. I then agreed to go with Sonny to the doctor's after supper. When Ma called Sonny, he reluctantly agreed to take me to the doctors, even though he would have rather gone to Armory Grill to play cards with his buddies. Thursday night was his night out with the guys. So after supper, Sonny took me to Dr. Kowlinger. Surprisingly, he didn't badger me with a million questions about my problem, which I was reluctant to discuss anyway.

In fact, since he came home from the service he rarely talked to me even when he lived with us. Although he was my big brother, we didn't have much of a relationship because he was away most of my younger life. But he did teach me how to oil my glove for little league and gave me that magical baseball signed by Mickey Mantle that I ruined playing baseball against the steps.

It was around seven o'clock when the doctor opened the door and waved for me and Sonny to come in. "Sit down next to the desk, Herbert," Dr. Kowlenger said. He gestured for Sonny to take a stool near the door. Boy, was it hot in his office. Being an unusually cold night for this time of year, the doctor had turned the heat on for the comfort of his mostly elderly patients sitting in the waiting room.

"You must be Sonny," Dr. kowlenger smiled. "Your mother always speaks glowingly of you and how you were in the Honor Guard."

"Thank you, Doctor. Mothers tend to do that" he laughed back. "I was fortunate and honored to be picked."

"So, Herbert, what seems to be the problem you couldn't tell your mom about? She called here very worried about you."

I looked sheepishly at Sonny, still reluctant to talk about my fears. He just smiled and said, "Don't worry, Herbie, the doctor is here to help you."

With that little bit of encouragement, all my hypochondriasis flowed out of me. I rambled on about going to the bathroom at the State Theater and picking up a horrible disease; twirling and pulling out my hair; feeling guilty because I masturbated and believing God was punishing me. But worst of all: I was going to die like Al Capone.

I could see out of the corner of my eye that Dr. Kowlenger was glancing slyly at Sonny, who was trying his damnedest to avoid bursting into a fit of laughter. "Hum, that is very interesting" Dr. Kowlenger stated quizzically. "Has anyone ever explained sex to you, like your dad or your mom or your brothers?"

"Not specifically. But my older sisters and Ma's friends always talked about guys who mess around getting bathroom diseases."

"I see," said Dr. Kowlenger stroking his chin. "Very interesting," he said. "Hum, bathroom diseases? So that's what they call them."

"Yes, sir, they do."

"Well, let me check you out and make sure you don't have one of those "bathroom diseases." With a subtle grin to my brother, the doctor began his exam. First he checked my scalp to see if anything was rotting away up there that I wasn't able to see. "Your scalp looks pretty normal, a little dandruff and I do notice a little area of thinning, but that will fill back in once you stop pulling out your hair." Next he took my blood pressure and it was ok. He then checked my ears and throat and found them to be normal. The real scary part came next when he handed me a plastic cup with a lid on it and said: "Ok, Herbert, I want you to take this bottle, go into the bathroom, and pee in it until you reach the red line. Then put the cap on it and bring it back to me after you finish. Ok?"

"Yes, sir," I nervously mumbled back. As I closed the bathroom door, I could hear muffled laughter and wondered what was so funny. As the cup was filling up to the line, I wondered what the heck I was going to do now, because I couldn't stop peeing. Flummoxed because I didn't want to overflow the bottle and look like a fool, I hastily put it on the sink and quickly turned to the toilet to finish. However, as I turned I couldn't hold back and sprayed some on the hot radiator. As a burst of steam rose, I thought, "Oh boy', I hope he doesn't come in here. Now the room smells like the urinal at the State Theater without those little white ammonia discs to staunch the stench."

After I finished, I noticed that I had left a couple, dark, pecker tracks on my tan trousers. But there was nothing I could do about them now. The damage was already done. So I quickly closed the door behind me, immediately returned to the doctor's desk hoping he wouldn't notice my slightly soiled trousers, and handed him the three-quarter filled cup.

"Thank you, Herbert. Now before I check this sample under the microscope I want you to undo your trousers and pull them down along with your underwear."

"Yes, sir" I said nervously, thinking "Here it comes. Now he is really going to see this terrible disease I have." Beside the hair pulling, slimy goop on the roots, the itching and all, I had recently developed a slightly, reddish rash on the inside of my thighs. I had truly thought that rash was the beginning of the end for me. Noticing the rash, he asked me if I sweated a lot and I said, "Yes, I do."

"Ok, now, Herbert, I want you to turn your head away and cough when I tell you to. Ok?"

"Yes sir," I responded.

Then he pushed his hand into my crotch real hard and said, "Cough." I hacked out a painful cough and wondered: Why is he doing this? He then reached around to the other side of my groin and did the same painful maneuver eliciting another hacking response from me. Then he grabbed my pecker and balls and examined them as though he were a used car salesman checking out the hood ornaments that hung from my belly. That was a very uncomfortable first and hopefully last intrusion into the sacred vault where my family jewels resided. Now red in the face I didn't know what to expect next. "Ok, Herbert, you can pull up you trousers now."

I quickly pulled up my underwear and trousers and sat back in the chair, anxiously awaiting the outcome of the urine test the doctor was now conducting behind that secretive white curtain. Within a few short minutes that seemed like hours, the doctor came back to his desk to announce the verdict. Would it be my feared death sentence or an acquittal of all the false charges rummaging around in my fertile, young mind?

After scribbling notes for several minutes then writing out what appeared to be a prescription and a note for school, the doctor turned toward me with a sensitive smile and said, "Herbert, there is nothing wrong with you other than the fact that you have a slight case of jock itch on your thighs that was probably caused by excessive sweating. You don't have a "bathroom disease" as you feared. In fact, it is extremely rare, if not impossible to get those diseases from a toilet seat. You are actually in very good physical condition. You have no hernias so you can resume sports if you like."

Phew, my cluttered mind was beginning to clear and the irrational fears seemed to melt away within moments. A huge weight had been lifted away. Dr. Kowlenger then told me that he had a discussion with Sonny while I was in the bathroom, and that Sonny had agreed to talk to me about sex and how to protect myself from ever getting one of those dreaded diseases. "Is that ok with you, Herbert?"

"Yes, Sir, it is."

He then handed me a note for school and a prescription for an ointment to clear up the jock itch. He also gave me a sample tin of powder to put on my thighs before exercising to help prevent further rashes. He then laughingly told me to stop pulling my hair because, if I didn't, I would continue to get bald spots, and girls weren't too fond of bald-headed guys.

Sonny handed Dr. Kowlenger the five dollar bill Ma had given him to cover the office visit and thanked him for checking me out and off we went. On the way home, Sonny gave me an abbreviated summary of everything I needed to know about sex that he had learned while in the service. Most of it flew right over my head in the five minute trip home. But the main thing he stressed was to use a Trojan if I ever did end up having sex one day. (Funny how they named a condom after my city.)

Needless to say, Ma was relieved after Sonny took her aside and explained everything that went on at the doctors. He then headed up to the Armory Grill to see if he could still get into the card game with his buddies.

"Now do you feel better, Herbie?"

"Yes, Ma, I do."

"Good."

Although I was finally at ease regarding my health, I never did rejoin the football team that year because I didn't want to explain to my teammates how dumb I was. Plus, I didn't want to burden Ma about coming up with money to buy me one of those cool team jackets. I believed I would be looked down on if I was the only kid on the team without a jacket. So I sacrificed a potential NFL career over a mythical disease and a twenty dollar football jacket. However, I did try out for basketball again that year!

CHAPTER TWENTY-TWO

Tuck Mashington

I rarely saw Alan, Billy or Denny anymore once I started high school. But when I did, 1 loved listening to their often outrageous stories. A couple such stories Alan told me stick out in my mind. The summer before my junior year I ran into Alan one Friday night down at the Famous Lunch. I was going to have a couple dogs before heading over to Whitey's pool hall to meet Larry when I spotted Alan sitting in a corner booth near the juke box, so I meandered over to say hi. Apparently Alan was home on leave after having joined the Navy a year earlier. "Hey, Alan, how have you been? How is the Navy treating you?"

"Not bad. I have a couple years left and then I'm done. It feels great to be home for a few days though. After I finish these little puppies (referring to the three unfinished dogs on his plate), I'm headed over to my sister Patty's house to see the family. So, how are you doing, Herbie?" Alan asked.

"So, so. I'm going to be a junior this year. I'm also working part-time at the Hendrick Hudson Garage washing cars with my brother-in-law Andy. Boy, I miss you guys." I said. "I never see Billy Finch or Denny anymore. I loved the stories you guys use to tell me. Hey, did you hear Tuck's back in the slammer? He got into another battle down at the Dugout."

"Ha-ha. That's the first thing I heard when I got back in town. He's one tough SOB, but he always treated me good."

Tuck Mashington was one of the most feared guys in the city. He was a black man who often drank too much, and when he did, he'd usually end up in a barroom fight. In fact, he got arrested so many times that he had his own special cell reserved for him in the Rensselaer County Jail on Fifth Avenue. It was rumored that he actually killed a guy once but was never charged. Tuck feared no man. However, he did fear one woman: Mary, his wife.

Tuck lived in a three-story brownstone on Congress Street, right near the appliance store on Ferry and Congress. My sister Kathleen and her husband Steve lived on the first floor. She complained to Ma about all the battles Tuck and Mary had when they got drunk. It scared her half to death when the cops would come and drag Mary into one patrol car and haul her off to Central station, then load Tuck into another and rush him to Samaritan Hospital. His torso looked like a series of zippers from all the stab wounds she inflicted on him over the years. However, he never pressed charges against her and she never ended up in prison. Luckily, my sister only lived there a short time. She was able to get a basement apartment a few buildings down from the RPI approach and lived there for several years before finally settling in Mechanicville.

Alan proceeded to tell me how Tuck used to let him hang out around his house or down in the basement where Tuck held weekly card games with his black buddies. These games went on for years. Whitey Robitaille was also a friend of Alan's and loved to drink and gamble. He was several years older than Alan and usually hung out at The Emerald Club or Walsh's Grill in Troy, and on occasion he'd end up at the Dugout on Congress Street. In fact, that's where he first met Tuck. They became friends but were not "close" friends. So it's understandable that Tuck was a bit leery when Whitey showed up one Saturday night with Muff Branerman who lived in Green Island.

Allan went on to describe to me what happened that night. Whitey handed his five dollar buy-in to Rufus, a huge black bouncer assigned to the cellar door. The five dollars got you into the game and gave you discounted prices for the booze sold during the game.

"Muff and I Just leaned against the wall and watched the game," Alan said. Apparently, Whitey was pretty much in the bag when they arrived, so it didn't take him long to go over the edge after a few more beers. Whitey usually got belligerent when he was shit-faced and, true to form, he got totally out of control.

Whitey became enraged, Alan noted, after losing his second big pot in a row to a short, light skinned black guy name Charlie Tooms. Slamming his cards on the table, Whitey spouted, "You're a fucking, sand bagging nigger, Charlie!"

Before Whitey could utter another slur, Tuck stood up, grabbed Whitey by the throat, and whacked him in the snoot. Whitey landed in a heap on the floor, unconscious with blood pouring out of his nose. "Get your asses over here." Tuck said, motioning to Muff and me. Within a few minutes we had dragged Whitey out to the front stoop and tried to revive him with a wet wash cloth Tuck had given us. "Do you know why the fuck I did this, Alan?" Tuck asked.

"No, Tuck, Why?"

"If this asshole said one more word, he'd be a dead man. Those guys would have killed him. So get his sorry ass out of here and don't ever bring him back."

"No problem, Tuck, you'll never see us again," said Muff. We loaded Whitey into the back of Muff's red Ford Torino and took off before anything else happened.

"Holy shit, Alan, you must have been scared to death," I said. "Did Tuck ever let you come back?"

"I was scared," Alan Said. "I thought Tuck had killed him. But I also realized Tuck was right. You can't use that kind of language about black people, especially to their face. Whitey was known for acting like an idiot when drunk, but this time took the cake. Luckily, Tuck never held it against me and still let me hang out at his place. Oh, before I go, Herbie I have to tell you another quick story about Tuck," Alan said. "This one is even scarier."

"Ok, I can hardly wait to hear this one," I laughed.

"Well, this one took place in Tuck's basement too." Alan then gave a detailed account of what happened that night: Mary and Tuck had been drinking and fighting most of the day and were both pretty well soused by the time the card game was to begin. Mary was passed out on the sofa when Tuck finally staggered downstairs to set up the game. Tuck had sobered up a bit, but was still pissed at Mary. Alan arrived about eight and sat at one of the high top cocktail tables Tuck had recently stolen from a storage room at the Hendrick Hudson Hotel. Sitting at that high table allowed him to get a good look at the player's hands. He could see who was bluffing and who wasn't. Then he mentioned his big mistake when he asked how Mary was doing.

Tuck complained that "the bitch is passed out on the sofa," not realizing Mary had come down the stairs and was ominously standing in the doorway with a 22 revolver in her hand. "You bastard," Mary screamed. "I'm going to fuckin' kill you."

Alan continued to tell how within seconds guys were diving for cover, including himself, as Mary pointed the gun at Tuck. Pop! Pop! Pop! Three shots clanged off metal chairs the guys had been sitting on. Tuck dove at Mary as she fired off another shot, hitting him in the thigh. He collapsed in pain on top of her, knocking her out cold when she hit her head on the hard, oak floor molding.

Alan was scared shitless and thought, what the hell was he going to do now when Tuck yelled to Alan to get me out, quick. Tuck had wrapped the oversized red bandana he always wore on his head around his thigh to stanch the blood pouring out of his leg. He asked Alan to press hard to help slow the bleeding. Tuck had Alan wrap another towel around it and then they both stepped over Mary and headed upstairs to Alan's new used car with its beautiful white leather seats.

Tuck told Alan to drive to Watervliet where he knew a doctor who owed him some favors. Alan described how he raced like hell down Congress Street and over the Congress Street Bridge, and luckily didn't get stopped by the cops. Once in Watervliet, Tuck directed him through a series of alleys until they reached the back door of Dr. Aizee. Apparently Tuck had taken care of a few personal "issues" for the doctor, so he was sure he would be taken care of. Tuck came back out in a half-hour and told Alan to take him home, warning him not to tell anyone about what happened because he and Mary both would end up in jail. That was the last time, Alan said, that he ever ventured down there.

After hearing Alan's scary account, I asked what happened to Mary, was she ok?

"Oh, she was fine," answered Alan. "I heard from Tuck later on that she didn't even remember what happened. I guess she had a bad headache, but thought it was from all her drinking. She thought it was just a bad hangover."

"Thanks for the stories, Alan. I got to run before my friend Larry takes off on me. Let me know when you're back in town, ok?"

"I will."

CHAPTER TWENTY-THREE

Bigots! Who Knew?

In the spring of 1961, my junior year, I was going through another transitional period of what seemed like an endless adolescence. I was beginning to question relationships I had with my friends, family and faith. These transitions occurred, I believe, due to the inherent nature of how we grow as human beings. It seems the more we learn, the more we begin to question things we had always accepted on pure faith before: friendships, family relationships, religion and political views.

Although I love history now, it wasn't my forte in high school. Because of that, I was ignorant of things like the Holocaust. I also never realized that my school buddies and I may have unknowingly become bigots! How could this be? I'm not a bigot now, or at least I don't believe I am. I think since my high school years I have evolved.

As a kid I played with colored kids, Jewish kids and kids of various ethnic backgrounds and never thought anything of it. They were kids, period. As an adult I have worked closely with blacks, Jewish people, gays and diverse ethnic groups. I have found that most people I have known are decent hard-working people with many shared goals: To be successful through hard work, love of family, friends, God, and country.

I also realized over a lifetime that being rich doesn't mean having a lot of money. There are many people who have lots of money but are poor in life experiences. Many have empty lives but plenty of material things. I don't have a lot of money or material things. But I have had a rich life, filled with loving memories of my family, dysfunctional as it may have appeared at times, but a real family and wonderful friends. (By the way, is there any such thing as a functional family?)

Although I loved sports in high school as well as band and chorus, I never realized until now that I may have been subconsciously a little prejudiced against some of my black and Jewish friends. I was in chorus since grade school and continued to sing all the way through high school. Larry, Ronnie and I were in Miss Miller's music class as well as the boy's glee club. We were all pretty decent singers, and I think deep down we thought we were better than some of the other kids. We weren't, of course, but we thought we were.

Ms. Miller was one of my favorite teachers since grade school and I always respected and trusted her. I remember that in grade school she took me under her wing and made me the lead in our Christmas play "The Littlest Angel" and had recommended that I become a member of the All City Chorus. However, Dickie Tomain joined the chorus this year for some unknown reason and began to have an onerous influence over some of us. In retrospect, I believe he was a latent bully, but during his short time hanging out with us his true character as a bully became clear.

I've learned that bullies and bigots use catchy slogans and phrases to imbed their message in fertile minds. You see it today in thirty-second sound bites to sway public opinion on different political or social issues. As teenagers we were extremely vulnerable to those same techniques, but in a more low tech manner than today.

I remember when Tom Beresney, Dickie, Larry and I were playing cards at Tom's house while his mom was at bingo. We were finishing off a couple bottles of Ballantine Ale when Dickie started a racist rant, the likes of which I had never heard before. He joked about all the names people used to put down people of color. I won't list them all here because, sadly, you have probably heard them all at one time or another. However, there was one term he credited to Jewish people and said they used it to mock people of color. I had never heard it used before, and the several Jewish friends I'd known since little league never used it. He said Jews called colored people "Schvartze's." He then used what he thought was a cool Jewish accent to demonize them even further, butchering the term over and over. That incident would lie in the back of my mind for a long time. I couldn't understand why we had to be put through Dickie's stupid anti-social exercise that night. However, in time it would rear its ugly head again.

Billy Converse, a black kid I played football with and really liked, auditioned for the same solo spot for our spring concert the rest of us guys were auditioning for. The song we rehearsed was "Moon River," made famous by Andy Williams. However, as good as we thought we were, Billy bested us. He got the solo because of his great audition.

"This sucks," Dickie complained. "She only picked him because he's a Schvartze." Of course, that planted the seed in our minds that we hadn't auditioned poorly but got shut out because he was a colored kid and Ms. Miller liked colored kids better than us. That wasn't true, of course, If that were the case, why would she have picked me for the lead in the grade school? I'm not colored—except maybe in the summer when I get a tan. So knowing that, I had some serious doubts as to what Dickie was claiming. However, I didn't dare to openly disagree with him because some kids in class thought Dickie was right. I stayed cowardly silent on the matter but still wondered if he was right.

Peer pressure has a very strong influence on impressionable young minds. It can be an insidious form of bullying that rides beneath youthful consciousness. One problem with peer pressure is that you don't often recognize or resist it until it's too late. In some cases, people go through their entire lives influenced by peer or group pressures. Others are able to resist because of logic and life experiences.

Here is an example of how insidiously bigotry and Dickie's not so subtle brainwashing had tunneled its way into our formerly innocuous perceptions of other kids. There was a chubby, Jewish kid named Arnie Pluckman that none of my friends seemed to like—especially Dickie, who had recently starting hanging out with Beresney, Larry, Billy, and me. Dickie had a strong personality that always seemed to garner attention. "Arnie Pluckman is an arrogant, circumcised prick," Dickie declared out of the blue one day. Arnie did act a little arrogant at times, but what circumcision had to do with it was beyond me. Maybe Arnie seemed arrogant because he was so much smarter in math class than us, knew it, and tried to lord it over the rest of us. But that shouldn't be a reason to mock and demonize him because of his penile anatomy, faith or ethnicity.

However, sadly, we ended up becoming involved in one of the cruelest, insensitive acts anyone could inflict on a person of Jewish descent. We allowed Dickie to taunt Arnie because he was Jewish. But even worse, Dickie made up a hateful rhyme that we, in our ignorance, thought was funny at the time. I guess in our deluded minds his chanting of this rhyme was a means of stripping away some of Arnie's arrogance. Apparently, Dickie had heard some news reports on television about the trial of a guy named Adolph Eichmann. We had never heard of him but listened in rapt attention to Dickie's disparaging rant about Jewish people. He called them kykes and whined about how the Jewish kids in school got all the breaks because their parents were rich and owned all the businesses in town.

We were standing at the edge of the parking lot at the north end of school when Arnie fatefully walked by on his way home. That's when Dickie started his tirade. He chided us to chime in but we didn't, thankfully. However, we did laugh and smirk as Dickie began in his cynical rant. "We like Ike, he killed the kykes; we like Ike, he killed the kykes; we like Ike, he killed the kykes."

"Stop it. That's disgusting," Arnie yelled back.

"What's the matter fat, little Jew boy?" Dickie yelled at him. "You can't take a joke, you kyke." We all stood by as Arnie began to cry from Dickie's taunts.

"Stop it, please!" Arnie pleaded, as Dickie jumped in front of him, forcing him into the road as he tried to get by. By that time Larry, Billy and I had backed away, sensing Dickie had gone over the line when Arnie began to cry harder and a small crowd had gathered expecting a fight. However, none occurred, because within minutes two male teachers came upon the scene and broke it up.

"Who started this?" Mr. Galou our shop teacher asked Arnie, who was shaking and whimpering and afraid to speak.

"He did," Carla Handlesman bravely volunteered, pointing at Dickie. During the commotion Billy, Larry and I had slithered our way to the back of the crowd hoping no one noticed. But when Mr. Barman, our gym instructor, asked if anyone else was involved, Carla paused for a moment, peered through the crowd, then pointed at us. "I think they were involved too."

Glaring at us now, Mr. Barman shook his head and quipped, "It doesn't surprise me!" Apparently we weren't some of his favorites in gym class. "All four of you report to the Principal's office tomorrow morning at eight o'clock sharp."

"Oh, boy," I thought. "We are in deep trouble now. Why they heck did we listen to Dickie. We could get suspended over this stupid incident. Ma's going to kill me." I didn't tell Ma what happened when I got home that night. I was hoping that when we went to the principal's office we would just get a slap on the wrist, have to stay after school a couple hours, and write "we're sorry for laughing" a couple hundred times, like we had to do in grade school when we got into minor trouble.

It turned out that this wasn't minor trouble. It was a serious offense. Larry, Billy and I arrived a few minutes early and were told to sit on the benches that lined the north side of the office next to the "Brush's" office. (Our principal, Mr. Enfanto was affectionately called the "brush" or "Groucho" because of his thick, trimmed mustache and the fact he looked like Groucho Marx.) All three of us sat there stoically chewing our gum until Mrs. Rampart, guardian of the principal's office, demanded we stop. So, of course, we obliged. But when she turned her back to answer the telephone, we dutifully stuck our gum underneath the wooden bench where it would mature like hundreds of other slabs of sedimentary rocks ready to be unearthed by an RPI archaeology student.

After sitting for what seemed an eternal ten minutes, the principal's door opened and Arnie meekly came out, glanced at us and headed for class. Shortly after, a smiling Dickie came out with a folder in his hand. He leaned over toward us and whispered that he got a three-day suspension that would give him a long weekend. Gleefully he headed out the door. It seems that nothing the Brush said had fazed him. I guess he would always be a bigot and a bully and was proud of it. Then it was our turn. First Billy then Larry entered the office for a five-minute tongue lashing. They walked past me with sullen looks on their face and said nothing. Then it was my time to face the music.

"Mr. Hyde! How shocked I am to see you here this morning," Mr. Enfanto admonished as I entered his office and took my seat in front of him. "I had reports from Mr. Murray that you were beginning to show signs of improvement in all your core courses, and that you had done well on the standardized tests we just completed. God only knows why you became involved in this seedy episode with Mr. Tomain and poor Mr. Pluckman?" I felt trapped in a situation that I wasn't exactly sure how to handle, especially not knowing what Dickie, Billy and Larry had said before I was interviewed.

I stammered a bit before finally speaking, fearing that we may have been sandbagged as scapegoats by Dickie. "Well, Sir. We were just hanging out talking when Arnie walked by. Dickie had been telling jokes and stuff and started a chant he thought was funny about this guy named Ike. We thought it sounded funny too and were laughing, but Arnie got very upset about it for some reason."

"Hmm," the Brush murmured, as he leaned forward on his desk with his chin in his hands not three feet from my face. "Do you know what the Holocaust is, Mr. Hyde? Have you ever heard of it or studied it?"

"No, Sir," I honestly stated.

"Well, guess what? You are going to study it now! I could very easily suspend all of you fellows for being vile accomplices of Mr. Tomain, but I'm not. Instead you are going to have after school detention for the rest of this week, and you're going to research in our library exactly what happened during the Holocaust. Then you are going to write a five-page report and give it to Ms. Rogers next Monday. I will review your work personally and if I think you have learned and understand what horrible things occurred during the Holocaust, I will clear your record. Do you understand, Mr. Hyde?"

"Yes, Sir," I meekly replied.

"Good, now off to class."

When I caught up with Larry and Billy at lunch I realized we were all lucky to get off so lightly. Each of us got the same assignment, but Larry had a heads up on us because, being a reader, he had read some stuff about it before from a book his dad had. His dad was an avid reader and it kind of rubbed off on Larry. After pissing and moaning about having to do extra work, we settled into our usual lunch routine of taking our cartons of chocolate milk, tearing a piece of wrapper off our straws, wetting the other end in the milk, then blowing it up to the stucco ceiling of the cafeteria. There it would stick and become a temporary resident, along with dozens of other stalactites in our miniature stalactite community. Sort of like Howe's cavern, but less chilly.

I did complete my penance on time and I'm glad I did, because I learned of all the atrocities that were committed during that God-awful war. I now understood how painful it must have been to Arnie, whose grandparents, I later learned, had lived through the Holocaust. I turned in my report and my record was cleared and Ma knew nothing of what occurred. She just thought I finally had done some homework.

Although I can try to claim now that it was an act of ignorance and youthful exuberance at the time, doing what we did is something I have always regretted, especially after learning the history of what occurred during the Holocaust. In retrospect, acting as we did was inexcusable.

CHAPTER TWENTY-FOUR

Laura Bunson

Dickie Tomain had infiltrated our close knit group for a while, although he wasn't a real friend, just more of shallow acquaintance. However, he and his cousin Laura sure made things interesting for our little cadre of sex-deprived teenagers in the spring and summer of our junior year, especially me. I was in study hall in mid-May when Larry whispered to me. "You should have been at Ronnie's house Saturday."

"Why?" I asked.

"Dickie Tomain brought his cousin Laura over to meet us. She and her parents were in town visiting his mom and she was bored to death, so Dickie suggested that she could waste a couple hours goofing off with Ronnie's sister and us."

"What do you mean, goofing off?"

"Well, Ronnie's parents were out for the day, so Ronnie invited us over to listen to music and play cards. But when Dickie called to see if he could come over with his cousin Laura we all started drooling."

Apparently Dickie told them she was kind of a hottie and very, *very* friendly. So they jumped on the idea and conned Ronnie's sister Velma to go to the movies that afternoon before Dickie and Laura got there.

"So what happened?" I whispered back to Larry with bated breath.

"Well, we played poker—Strip poker!"

"Are you kidding me?" I laughed.

"Nope, I'm not kidding you."

Now I was really getting worked up thinking about what I had missed. "Damn it," I thought. "Why did I have to play in that ball game Saturday?" "So, did she go very far?" I urged Larry, who now had a huge grin on his face.

"Man, she was pretty and had a great set of boobs."

"You saw her boobs?" I said panting.

"Well, not exactly," he sheepishly replied.

"What do you mean, not exactly?" Now I was flummoxed.

"Well, she was a real good poker player," Larry cringed, "She didn't lose a hand for over a half hour, and before we knew it she had Billie, Ronnie and me down to our skivvies."

"What about Dickie? Was he down to his skivvies too?"

"Nah, he didn't play since it was his cousin. He just sat in the corner laughing his ass off as we got our clocks cleaned by Laura."

"Keep it down, Herbert," Mrs. Fauxwald, our English and study hall teacher, yelled when she heard me laughing uncontrollably.

"Yes, Ma'm." I said, struggling to stop laughing.

"Dickhead!" Larry spouted back at me under his breath. "It wasn't that funny. It was embarrassing losing to her. But we did finally win a few hands and got her to unbutton a couple buttons on her blouse!"

"Wow," I whispered back. "You're one lucky son-of-a-gun; you almost saw her boobs," I laughed. I then mumbled, with a twinge of sarcasm, hoping Mrs. Fauxwald wouldn't hear me; "That's as far as you got?"

"She would have gone all the way," Larry insisted, trying to counter my teasing, "but Ronnie's sister came home unexpectedly. It's a good thing Dickie spotted her walking up the street otherwise we could have been caught with our pants down."

"Boy, I guess you were lucky," I smirked.

"But guess what?" Larry whispered, "We're going bowling next Saturday at the Bowlatorium, and Laura is coming with Dickie."

"Great!" I exclaimed. "I can come and meet her!"

"After busting my balls, you think we should let you come? I don't think so," Larry sniped. But after a few minutes he reconsidered. "You can come as long as you bring enough money. We reserved a couple lanes for 1:30 with Art."

"Ok, I'll see if I can scrounge up the money." I figured I would have to come up with about three or four bucks to pay for my bowling and a soda or two. Whack! I felt a sharp, burning sting in back of my left ear. It quickly subsided as I looked up and saw Mrs. Fauxwald hovering over me with her weapon of choice, a sharpened number two pencil, with the eraser ominously poised to strike again.

"What did I tell you about talking in study hall, Mr. Hyde?"

"No talking," I whimpered in response, "I won't do it again."

"You better not!" she glared over her half, rimmed glasses. "I may have a little trouble hearing (she wore two hearing aids) but I could hear you out on Burdett Avenue."

"Boy, I hope she didn't hear everything," I thought to myself. I acutely remembered what happened with a sharpened number two pencil, "Ivanhoe" and Dick Cross my freshman year.

The next Saturday I arrived early for bowling with four and a half dollars in my pocket. I figured that would be more than enough to rent shoes, buy a burger, fries and a soda, and bowl three games. Art was already bowling on the alley closest to the snack bar. He was such a great bowler and would become one of the best in the area as time went on. He had become addicted to bowling after coming here with Larry, Billy and me a year or so earlier. In fact, that's why he took a job here: he would get paid for maintaining the lanes, equipment and shoes, and get as much free bowling as he could handle. "Hi, Art. How are you hitting' em today?"

"Hi, Herbie," Art replied. "I'm not hitting them good at all. Last night I only rolled a five eighty-five in my spring league. I should have rolled a solid six hundred. I have to keep practicing so I can bowl on Howard Tupper's TV Tournament Time someday."

Art was a left hander and had a natural hook. He perfected it so well that he was in the pocket 95% of the time. I, on the other hand, was right handed, and perfected my non-hook so well that I was in the pocket about 59% of the time. Wonder why I averaged around one forty, while Art was always in the two hundreds.

"I can't wait for the guys to come with Dickie's cousin. Have you met her yet, Art?"

Art smirked and replied, "Not yet, but I hear she is quite a girl. Billy said she is looking forward to meeting you."

"Really, Art?" I blurted in surprise. "Hum. I wonder what they were saying about me to her—nothing good, I bet."

Art laughed outloud and replied, "They would never say anything bad about you, Herbie, ha, ha. You guys are always busting on each other. Knowing Billy, he probably told her you were hung like a mule."

"Yea," I laughed back, "a miniature mule."

Art finished his practice game then went behind the counter to find a pair of nine and a half bowling shoes for me just as Larry and Billy arrived. Billy came over and goosed me like he used to in grade school, then laughed and said, "Still hung like a mule."

I looked at him befuddled as I knocked his hand away, and seriously began to wonder if he had said something stupid to Laura, and that's why she wanted to meet me. "Nah, he wouldn't do that, would he?" I thought. But before I could say anything more or whack him in the nuts, Dickie appeared at the door. Beside him was a pretty girl with light brown hair and powder blue eyes. She was wearing a white, button down blouse, a tan, v-neck sweater that seemed to be bulging at the seams, and a pair of tight fitting blue jeans.

"Wow", I thought to myself, "she is so pretty." I quickly became enamored of her.

"Hi, Herbie", Laura said with a soft, sultry voice. "I've heard a lot about you." She then leaned forward and gave me a hug and a huge smile. I was beside myself as my hormones began to dance the cha cha.

Art soon came over and said he had set up two lanes for us: Lane twenty-six for me, Laura, Larry and Billy; lane twenty-five for Dickie and him. As soon as we had picked out our house balls and had settled in our seats, Billy took it upon himself to make up teams. He and Larry were going to play Laura and me. Being so competitive, I guess he figured he would rather wipe up the floor with me than try to make out with Laura. That put Larry in an awkward position because I think he wanted to hit on Laura, and now it would be more difficult since she was sitting right next to me. In fact, she was so close to me that she was almost sitting on my lap. I was actually starting to feel a bit uncomfortable with her so close. I wasn't used to that. But she did smell nice. She must have been wearing Avon or something. "Boy", I thought. "I hope I don't have BO." I was really worried, even though I had taken a bath that morning.

"Ok. The losers of the first game buy the winners a Coke," Billy declared.

I reluctantly agreed but worried that I didn't have much money on me if we lost. I had paid for my games and had ordered a Coke and some fries so my resources were running low. Luckily, Laura had paid for her own stuff before we got started. "Ok." I responded, figuring I could afford it, especially if Laura paid her portion of the bet. (However, I didn't realize she probably expected me to pay.) Billy sat at the scorer's table keeping score. Thank God for that because I could never figure out how to do it, being so great in math in all.

Surprisingly, Laura started off with a spare. In fact, she was a very good bowler. After the first frame she whispered in my ear that she was on her high school bowling team. She then put her arm around my shoulders and nuzzled my neck as we watched Larry throw a gutter ball right after whacking himself in the ankle. No one had ever nuzzled my neck before. I was now entering a hormonal place I'd never been before.

"Damn, that hurts," Larry whined to Billy as he limped back to his seat. Billy just looked at him in disgust, realizing that they were in trouble. I was actually shooting a decent game, while Laura was twenty points better than all of us going into the eighth frame. While Billy and Larry were shooting themselves in the foot that first game, Laura was all over me for some reason. She was hugging me and kissing my cheek and neck every time she came back to her seat. Now I was starting to get red in the face and began sweating. But worst of all, my mini-mule was beginning to get restless. I struggled to keep him under control each time I had to stand up and bowl.

"Why are you hunched over like that, Herbie?" Billy quipped. He knew exactly what my problem was.

"It's the way I always bowl, "I fired back.

"No it's not, you look weird," Billy laughed. "Straighten up and bowl like a man."

Luckily, it was the tenth frame and I got a strike on my first ball. That gave me a chance to calm things down as I backed up toward the ball return. I ended up shooting a one thirty-five while Laura shot a one sixty-five. Larry shot a one nineteen while Billy beat me shooting one thirty-eight. We won thanks to Laura's great game so I was able to save what little money I had left. Because they lost the first game so badly, Billy decided it wasn't wise to bet on the remaining two games. So there wasn't any more pressure about my running out of money. I then ordered some fries which I shared with Laura, but that pretty much wiped out my funds leaving me with seventy-five cents to my name.

As we were finishing our last game, Billy suggested we all go to the Palace Diner for the high school special served every Saturday afternoon: cheeseburger with gravy fries and a Coke for $2.50. Billy said that they were going to meet Tom Beresney there after bowling. He couldn't make it for bowling but wanted desperately to meet Laura. After changing my shoes, I cornered Billy out of

ear shot of Laura and told him that I couldn't go to the Palace. I'd
wiped out the money I brought bowling. I was broke.

"Boy, that was dumb," Billy lamented. "I can't help you. I've got
just enough money for myself."

"No problem. I'll just tell her I have to go home to help move
some furniture or something." It was soon after that I saw Billy,
Larry, and Dickie outside yakking and laughing about something.
Then they pointed at me and Laura as we huddled inside the vestibule.

"What the heck are they talking about, Herbie?" Laura asked as
she began snuggling against my chest.

"They're just whining about you beating them. You're one heck
of a bowler."

"Thanks," Laura smiled.

When I looked up again, all three guys were across the street
talking to Tom Beresney who had just gotten off the bus in front
of the diner. Now I wondered what the heck they were all laughing
at. No doubt they were laughing at me. Soon they began waving
and yelling to Laura to get over there and meet Beresney. Boy, that
really made me feel great, especially since I had now become so
enamored of Laura.

Out of the blue Laura hugged me so tight that I thought I'd
stop breathing. She then kissed me and whispered in my ear as
she grabbed my crotch, "Hmm, Billy has a point." Like a lightning
bolt she flashed out the door, leaving me and my hormones standing at attention as she raced over to meet Beresney. That was
the first and last time I ever saw Laura. However, Ronnie filled
me in later that he had seen her and Tommy making out near
Ned Abbott's store a couple weeks later. This ordeal with Laura
turned out to be the continuation of a sad pattern of debacles
I endured with girls during high school, starting with my freshman dance when I was turned down by Sharon Manderville. I was
beginning to feel like a freak, unable to establish a relationship

with any girl, while most of my male buddies had already ended up with a girlfriend or had reached the ultimate pinnacle all male youth strive for. (I'll let you figure out what *that* means!)

CHAPTER TWENTY-FIVE

Popping, Fresh Dickie Tomain

As most of you are aware, kids have snuck into movies since the advent of movie theaters. We were no exception. As a young kid growing up on the corner of College and Eighth, I had plenty of experience sneaking into just about every theater in Troy with my buddies. They were pros. As high school students, we didn't do it quite as much but still managed on occasion to sneak into my favorite, the magnificent Troy Theater on River Street adjacent to the Mayflower Restaurant. We had to be a bit more sophisticated when sneaking into the Troy Theater than the other theaters. The box office was situated on River Street at such an angle that the ticket sellers could see who was on the street as well as who was hanging out in the elongated vestibule that led up to the carpeted lobby and concession area. On the west side of the concession area was a beautiful, marble staircase leading to the balcony. On either side of the staircase were steps that led down to the main seating area.

Several times earlier we had taken advantage of young ticket takers who worked the weekend matinee shift by trying to intimidate and confuse them in order to sneak in. One of our buddies, who didn't really want to go to the show, would get into an argument over a supposed lost ticket and while he was distracting the naïve ticket taker, the rest of us would quietly rush through the door furthest from the action and take up seats on opposite sides of the theater. If no one came to check for tickets, we were home safe. We would then sit together and watch the show.

However, that particular charade didn't always work as planned. The last time we tried it we got caught by the weekend manager. He saw what we had done and then approached us once the movie started. He shined his flashlight in our face and asked for our tickets, and when we couldn't produce them, he summarily marched us out like common criminals and warned us not to try it again or he'd turn us in to the cops. Well, that scared us for a while, until we learned that the manager had taken a new job in Albany. We also heard that they had hired an old, gray-haired guy to take tickets for the weekend matinees. In fact, some kids had complained that he yakked so much that sometimes the ticket line would be backed up almost all the way to the ticket window.

Billy, Larry, Dickie and I were sitting in the Mayflower around noon on Saturday trying to figure out how to kill some time that afternoon. We didn't feel like walking all the way to the Bowlatorium and hanging out with Billy's brother Art, so we decided to go to the movies instead. Dickie suggested that maybe we could get lucky with some hot girls in the balcony where they usually hung out. It was right after that statement that he laughingly told us a joke he heard recently during a party at his uncle's house. Dickie usually wasn't too good at telling jokes but we listened intently anyway.

It was a tale about how a young man had taken a woman to the movie on their first date. He was really attracted to her, but she was kind of ignoring him during most of the romantic scenes. He had bought a box of popcorn which he was holding in his lap, when suddenly he developed an erection he couldn't contain and didn't want to waste. Somehow he was strategically able to push it through the bottom of the box unbeknown to her. When he offered her some popcorn, she reached in and got a handful of penis at the same time. She was shocked at first, but he was successfully able to explain to her that he was so aroused by her beauty that he couldn't contain himself.

"The end result," Dickie laughed, "She soon had a handful of buttered popcorn." We all laughed hysterically at the punch line but told Dickie that it was ridiculous, and that no one would ever have the guts to pull off a stupid stunt like that. With that said, we all pooled our money in order to buy one ticket so the rest of us could sneak into the matinee. We each coughed up fifty cents, which would cover the seventy-five cents for one ticket, plus a dollar and a quarter for a large box of popcorn we could all share. That was quite a bargain for our fifty-cent investment.

We elected Larry to buy the ticket and distract the old codger who was taking tickets. It worked like a charm. In fact, it almost worked too well for Larry, because by the time the guy shut up Dickie had already bought a large box of popcorn, about the size of a cereal box, and we were safely nestled into our comfy seats in the balcony waiting for the movie to start. Larry fumbled his way to his seat next to me all the while complaining, "That's the last time I'm going to do that. The old guy wouldn't shut up. I thought my ears were going to start bleeding."

Billy leaned over and whispered to Larry," Stop your whining. Now you know how I feel when you get going."

"Dickhead," Larry shot back.

"Pussy," Billy laughed as several of the girls turned around, shocked by what they heard as they waited for the show to start.

Billy waved and smiled at the girls who had turned around and a couple actually smiled back at him. They were all about our age. Billy then leaned over and said to us boasting, "I think the blond has the hot's for me. She wants my body."

"I doubt that," Larry snapped back. "You couldn't get laid at Mame Faye's with a fistful of hundreds."

"Too bad Mame's isn't around anymore," Dickie lamented.

Their blather continued for several minutes until the lights finally dimmed and the cartoons started—the usual fare of Wile E. Coyote followed by Sylvester and Tweety bird. Finally the feature began, a boring love story about eating Breakfast at Tiffany's Jewelry Store or something like that. We paid little attention to the movie and focused most of our attention on the cute girls in front of us. As the movie went on, our boredom increased, until Dickie started pelting the girls softly with popcorn to get their attention. They ignored it at first, but after a while several got annoyed and moved further away, leaving a couple empty seats next to the two cutest girls who had smiled earlier.

"Hey, Billy," Dickie said, "I bet I can pull off that popcorn stunt I told you about."

"What are you, nuts?" Larry and I said in unison. "You'll get us all arrested and I don't want nothing to do with that," I whined, scared to death he would do it. That's when Larry and I looked at each, nodded, and decided to high tail it out of there before Dickie went over the edge. As we headed up the ramp to the exit doors and lobby, we heard Billy teasing Dickie.

"You ain't got the nerve, Dickie, you ain't got the nerve."

Shortly after Billy caught up to us, warning that we had better get the hell out of there, quick. "Why?" Larry uttered with concern.

"The crazy bastard's going to do it. He is actually going to do it! I saw him put it in the bottom of the box."

Within seconds we heard girls screaming at the top of their lungs as ushers raced in to see what was going on. We looked back and there was Dickie running like crazy, popcorn flying all over the place with the new manager nipping at his heels. Larry, Billy and I quickly headed south towards Whitey's pool hall as Dickie headed north toward Franklin Square where he quickly disappeared into the large crowd of Saturday shoppers.

We stayed at Whitey's for an hour or so shooting pool until we figured the coast was clear. Luckily, Dickie didn't get caught and nothing more came of it. The next time we saw Dickie was when we were all hanging out at Frear Park. It was getting dusk out as we finished a pick-up basketball game. A neighbor kid from Tenth Street by the name of Jim Lucie played with us that night. He was kind of chubby and was an easy target to tease.

So, of course, Dickie decided to make a fool of him after I refused to let them "de-pant" me by pushing him away. Jimmy couldn't, so within about a minute he had Jimmy's khaki's hanging about ten feet up on one of those iron cleats the linemen use to make repairs, directly under the street light so everyone passing by could see him in his skivees. Poor Jimmy had the toughest time getting them down and vowed to get revenge somehow, someway. However, I'm not sure he did get his revenge.

After this last, stupid, cruel incident, Dickie vanished from the scene. Not seeing him around raised questions as to what happened to him. From what I heard in the cafeteria, his parents had somehow gotten wind of his hijinks and decided to pull him out of school. We also learned through the grapevine that his family moved out of the area shortly after, and that was a good thing because he was going to be expelled permanently from school. Apparently Jimmy's parents found out what Dickie had done to their son from some neighbors who had seen the incident at Frear Park. That, coupled with other nasty things he incited at school, was more than enough to justify his expulsion.

CHAPTER TWENTY-SIX

Hi Tech: The Scanner, The Times Are Changing

During high school things really began to change in both my family and the neighborhood. I began to realize Ma was a real worrywart about her children, even her adult children. She undoubtedly had good reason with my brother Cliff and me. But I never realized how much she worried about my brother Sonny until Dorothy bought Mom a scanner for Christmas—just around the same time Sonny became a fireman. I think I inherited that worrywart trait from her because I constantly worry about my family's health, safety and welfare today.

I remember waking up during a hot summer night and seeing Ma silhouetted against a moonlight sky, slumped forward in her arm chair, woefully listening as the scanner lights blinked between static-filled calls from Central Station. In the distance I heard sirens eerily wailing. She always listened to them late at night, especially on the nights Sonny was working. I can easily imagine her fear when reports came over the air that a firefighter was down during a major blaze. In fact, Sonny was injured during several fires. During one of those blazes, a ceiling beam collapsed on top of him, knocking him unconscious. He was pulled from this inferno by his fellow squad members before the rest of the ceiling gave way. Luckily, he only suffered a minor concussion. Every time a firefighter rushes into a blaze he is putting his life on the line, and Ma feared in her heart Sonny could be killed or maimed for life. She never overtly mentioned this to anyone, but on this night I could sense everything she was feeling.

It was rare during high school that I stayed out late, except maybe on the weekends when I would come strolling in well after midnight. As I remember now, Ma always seemed to be up when I got home, unable to sleep until she knew I was safely home. She never yelled at me, but I began to notice additional wrinkles developing under her beautiful blue eyes. I know now that I must have been part of the cause of those wrinkles. As kids, and especially as teenagers, we rarely see beyond what we deem important to us. We aren't concerned about our parents' concerns. Teenagers can be selfish, self–absorbed snots and I apparently fit quite comfortably into that mode.

A lot of transitional things occurred during the latter part of grade school and continued through high school. As my older brothers and sisters married and started families, we began to have more family events. In my younger years most social things we did during the summer were with our neighbors: Summer plays in Pete Fermetti's back yard, neighborhood picnics at White Bridge, and watching beer baseball games our neighbors played at School Fourteen field.

It was during this period that we began our traditional family picnic each Fourth of July at Pine Lake, an area located north of Valley Falls near Johnsonville, were we enjoyed a small pond, campground and picnic pavilion. Kathleen and Steve would get up early in the morning and reserve several picnic tables and parking spots for us. It was easy for them to do because each year they rented a camp from the Cephol family. The Cephols also owned the enclosed pavilion at the lake and ran the snack bar.

Dorothy and Jimmy and Patty and Andy loaded up their trunks with food and goodies for the day, along with lawn chairs so that Ma wouldn't have to sit at the cramped picnic tables all day while we kids swam in the lake. Sonny and Marge came once in a while too. We played pick-up baseball games horseshoes and, of course, there was always bingo...another boring game I love to hate. On rare occasions even my brother Jack would drag his family down from Bennington for the day.

The fourth of July seemed exhausting for Ma. I know she loved seeing all her kids and grandkids, but by the end of an oppressively hot day, she looked drawn and frazzled. She usually tried to sit under a shady tree most of the day, but there was little escape from the late afternoon sun once bingo started. Her only respite from the oppressive heat was Andy's humorous bingo calling. Ma got the biggest kick out of listening to him struggle to speak English with his acute Abenaki/Canadian accent. Whenever he had a number under the letter B, all hell broke loose. "Ok, next number is, A Beeta-one." Andy shouted above the laughter.

"When the hell are you going to learn to speak English, you crazy Canuck?" my brother Cliff would yell at him. That started the ball rolling. Now every other number Andy messed up would cause an outburst of laughter that amused even Andy. I honestly think he used to butcher the calls on purpose in order to generate those laughs. Andy was a pretty shrewd guy and always seemed to be the big winner at the end of these games. I think his Abenaki nickname must have been "sly dog." At dusk when the bingo games ended, we all helped clean up our garbage, loaded the cars back up with leftover goodies and the kids, and meandered home.

I remember coming home from one of those Fourth of July picnics that was stifling hot even at eleven o'clock at night, driving Ma, Patty and me to sit on the front porch in a vain attempt to cool off. Patty and Ma were drinking cokes, smoking their Chesterfields and complaining about the heat, as well as the sad fact we were losing our neighbors in droves. Desperately, we tried to inhale every slight breeze that skittered by us.

Patty and Andy now lived on the first floor of the Gibson's house while we lived on the second floor. Thank God, Dorothy and Jimmy were able to purchase the house the previous year so we all had a place to live after Dad left us to fend for ourselves. Typically around 11:30 Tony Fermetti pulled up in his brand new red Chevy Impala. He recently bought it from the spoils he earned from working his butt off at his brother Frank's insurance company. Looking up as he locked the door on his new "Babe Mobil'e" he waved furiously at Ma and yelled, "How are you, Mabel? Have you got a cold one for me?"

"Sure, come on up," Ma, laughed. She then whispered to Patty, "He thinks we have a beer for him."

That's when Patty yelled, "Don't cater to him, Ma. He still thinks he's the Don Juan of Eighth Street. Just ask Eva Belle Smithers if you don't believe me."

"That's old news, Patty Cakes" Tony replied as he headed across the street.

"Herbie, quick, go ask Andy for a Coke." Patty cackled. "Better still," she whispered, "get three—two cold and one warm."

"Ok, Patty, but can I have another too?"

"No! You still have half a bottle left."

"Darn," I whined as I went into their apartment.

Whenever Tony came over he'd humorously brag about his sexual escapades and conquests, real or imagined, and this always set Patty off on a tangent. I could never figure out if Patty was serious or kidding when she busted Tony's chops. By the time I returned with the sodas, Tony was gently pinching and twisting the dimples on Ma's cheeks, a ritual he performed every time he came over when we were sitting on the porch. Ma feigned being in pain as she slapped his hands away. She then grabbed both of his cheeks and really squeezed them. Within seconds he was begging for mercy. "That will teach you!" Patty laughed as Tony rubbed his now red cheeks.

"Jesus, Mabel that hurt like hell," Tony whimpered. "You're the toughest woman I ever met."

"So how is the new car, Romeo?" Patty quipped.

"It's great, a real babe magnet."

"Yea, right," Patty sniped. "The only thing you could pick up with that car is a case of the cooties."

"Oh really, Patty? Do you want take a ride up to the park and check out my cooties?"

"Stop your joking, Tony. You know she is a married woman now," Ma smirked.

"I know, Mabel." Tony laughed. "I just wanted to find out if she still has cooties."

"You're cruising for a bruising, you dumb Dago," Patty sniped back. Even Andy, who had just come out on the porch with a can of beer in his hand laughed. That's when Patty handed Tony the warm bottle of Coke, and gave Ma one of the cold ones.

Looking at the cold beer in Andy's hand, Tony complained, "Hey, where's my cold beer?"

"Sorry, Tony, this is the last one," Andy quipped in his best French Canadian accent.

"Geeze, I walked all the way up here and all I get is a piss warm bottle of Coke, and two bruised cheeks."

Everyone laughed except Tony who feigned being emotionally distraught by the slight he received. That's when Andy handed the just-opened can and gave it to Tony. "You can have mine, we have plenty inside," Andy laughed.

"Thanks, Andy. I don't care what they say about you crazy Indians and fire water. At least you're willing to share yours."

Tony stayed for about a half-hour commiserating with us about losing our friends and how our neighborhood was slowly disappearing. No longer could Ma sit with Helen or Winnie since they had moved away. Those moves had created a social void as well as an emotional void in Ma's heart. They were her friends and she missed them dearly. Luckily, on rare occasions, Virginia Perrault or Jeannie Lempki would stop over and sit on the porch and keep Ma company.

Before Tony left, he couldn't help but regale us with stories about my father and his artificial leg. The older kids had given him the nickname "High Speed" in describing how fast he hobbled his way down to Stickley's grill on the corner of Congress Street and Rock Alley to get his daily ration of beer or how he would try to chase after them when they purposely knocked over some of his Christmas trees in the lot behind the Bassett building to bust his chops. I guess my Dad must have been pretty miserable to some of those guys. Otherwise why do something so mean to him?

Ma treated Tony like another son, and I think that bothered Patty for some reason when she was younger. On any given morning I'd wake up and see Tony sitting at our kitchen table smoking and doing the daily racing form while drinking a cup of Ma's coffee, oblivious to what was going on around him. Tony loved to play the horses and numbers and often went to the track or placed his bets with one of the ubiquitous bookies downtown. One morning when Patty was still in high school, for some unknown reason she snuck up behind Tony unseen and lit his paper on fire. Still immersed in his daily picks, Tony never noticed the additional smoke wafting around the room until the flames reached his finger. That's when he screeched at Patty as she doused his paper with a cup of water. "You crazy shit Patty, What the hell's the matter with you?"

"That'll teach you to drink all our coffee. You don't live here and it's not a restaurant."

"Geez, I'll pay for the coffee if that makes you happy," Tony whined as he held a piece of ice Ma had given him to treat his slightly burned finger.

"Patty, that was uncalled for. Tony is always welcome here, so don't you ever do that again," scolded Ma.

"Well, I'm just sick of him being around, especially when I'm not feeling well."

"Then go to your room until you feel better," chided Ma. That's when Patty stomped into her room, mumbling to herself. Ma then looked at Tony with a quirky smile and whispered, "It's that damned curse. She didn't mean what she said. Besides, I think she has a little crush on you."

"Well, that's a funny way of showing it, Mabel. But I forgive her...now if she were a couple years older I'd..."

"Stop it right now, Tony", Ma laughed. "Those kind of silly remarks always get you in trouble."

CHAPTER TWENTY-SEVEN

My Worst Sunburn in History

Kathleen and Steve rented a camp each year for their four kids, Stevie, David, Susie and Wendy and invited one or two of us kids to spend a week with them during the summer. When Patty was younger, she usually stayed a week. So did my sister Brenda who always loved camping and as an adult often traveled across the country with her husband Jim in their travel-trailer. Her kids also became camping addicts and to this day still love to camp.

Me on the other hand, not so much. I don't like the rustic life style: the heat, mosquitos, flies, poison ivy, dirt and outhouses. I never enjoyed swatting flies at dinner or lunch, whether in our oppressive third floor tenement or the open air of the great outdoors. So I never really cared if I was invited to Kathleen and Steve's camp. However, during the late summer of my freshman year I finally gave in and decided to spend a weekend there. Steve picked me up that Friday afternoon on his way home from work at the Star Woolen Plant in Cohoes where he was a supervisor. I packed a couple pair of underwear, socks, tee shirts and my bathing suit.

Steve, who was usually pretty quiet, was very talkative on the way out to the lake. "You're going to have a great time this weekend, Herbie. The weather is going to be great and you can walk over to the pavilion tonight and listen to the jukebox if you get bored. There are usually lots of kids your age over there on Friday nights," Steve said.

I liked Steve and remembered how a couple years earlier how he had taken me fishing on the Hudson near Mechanicville, where they lived. I had only really fished once in my life with my dad when I was really young. The times I fished with Alan down by the river don't count because we didn't have real fishing poles. Consequently, I was a very inexperienced fisherman. Steve baited my hook for me like my dad had done and showed me how to cast. We were fishing for a fish he called a bull-head, which intrigued me. I wondered if it had horns sticking out of the sides of its head like a steer. Steve attached a lead sinker to each of our lines so they would sink to the bottom of the river. These fish were bottom feeders, I guess.

We weren't catching anything and I was getting bored, so Steve told me to just sit on a huge boulder in back of him for a little longer. If he didn't catch anything soon, we'd head home. After about ten minutes Steve leaned back to make his final cast. Bam, I felt a horrible, burning pain in the back of my head. I screeched and cried with pain. Poor Steve was beside himself. On his last cast, he had inadvertently whacked me in the head with the biggest sinker in the world. A huge lump at the base of my skull was throbbing with pain and turning red. Steve had ice in his cooler and quickly put a cold compress on the back of my head. Luckily, I didn't have to go to the hospital or suffer any major damage that I hadn't already incurred during my young life. To this day I still have a small hard lump on the back of my head about the size of a knuckle. I guess that's why I act like a knuckle head at times.

We soon passed the pavilion and headed toward their campsite on the northern edge of the lake. The dirt road that led to the site was full of ruts and tree roots which made the ride even more challenging to the car's suspension. Each time we bottomed out, I whacked my head on the padded interior of the car's roof. Although their site appeared hidden from the roadway, they had a great view of the lake between the two fifty-foot pine trees that provided shade and privacy. They also had a small sandy area near the shore that they used as their own private beach.

"Hi, Herbie," Kathleen said as I lumbered out of the car rubbing the top of my head. "Bumpy ride, Herbie?" She laughed, knowing full well how treacherous the road was.

"Just a little," I complained. "Next time I'm wearing my football helmet."

That's when Steve laughed and tossed my gym bag at me. "I knew you'd survive, Herbie," Steve laughed. "What's for dinner, Hon?" Steve asked Kathleen. "I'm starving."

"I made macaroni salad and marinated that big steak we brought. Once you get the charcoal going, I'll cook the corn."

There was a big pot of water already boiling on a huge Coleman stove outside near their clapboard cabin. Inside the four-bedroom camp I could hear young Stevie and Susie arguing over who cheated playing pickup sticks. It sounded eerily similar to how my sisters and I argued over all the silly games we played as kids. I guess arguing over stupid stuff must be imbedded deeply in Hyde DNA. "Herbie, you can put your stuff in the bedroom on the left with the yellow curtain," Kathleen said as I opened the rickety screen door. Each tiny bedroom had a different colored curtain covering the door for privacy.

"Ok", I replied, stumbling over pickup sticks scattered across the wooden plank floor.

"Hi, Uncle Herbie. Stevie cheated," Suzie whimpered with an alligator tear welling up in the corner of her eye.

"No, I didn't!" Stevie emphatically replied. "You're just a sore loser, Suzie."

That's when Suzie burst into a full blown meltdown and ran out crying to Kathleen. "Stevie's picking on me and called me a loser, Ma."

Within seconds Kathleen was in the kitchen with Suzie in tow and scolded Stevie, "Stop picking on your little sister, and Suzie, stop whining, ok?"

"But, Ma, he cheated," Suzie implored.

"No, I didn't" Stevie fired back. "She's just a bad loser."

"All right, stop it, both of you. I've had enough of this. Susie, put the game away and go to your room until dinner is ready. Stevie, take the garbage down to the dumpster then come back and help your dad outside." I just stood there and looked on in amazement. Kathleen looked and acted so much like Ma as memories of my early childhood flashed in front of my eyes. I realize now that we always had strong women in our family.

Dinner was terrific: barbecued steak, corn on the cob, macaroni salad and a big slice of watermelon. Kathleen was a great cook like Ma. I was stuffed by the end of dinner and decided to take Steve's advice and headed over to the pavilion as the sky was getting dusky looking outside. When I pushed open the weathered screen door to the pavilion, I heard raucous laughter erupting from a group of kids at the other end of the building near the jukebox. I bought a Coke at the concession then wandered over near where the group was huddled, intrigued to find out what was going on.

I took a seat on the corner of a wooden picnic table near the rear entrance and adjacent to the neon lit jukebox. I was just close enough to listen in on what all the laughter was about. There were five guys my age and three girls in their early teens. One girl in particular seemed to garner most of the attention. She was a very pretty, petite blond with greenish, hazel eyes and had her hair pulled back into a pony tail. She seemed to be relishing most of the testosterone- driven attention from what appeared to be a bunch of local yokels. She abruptly got up from the group and headed over to the jukebox as the others walked up to the counter to get some sodas and snacks. She was immediately stalked by a scruffy looking guy at the urging of the group.

Come on, Colleen, I want the next slow dance with you?" chirped the freckle-faced, brush cut kid in farmer jeans. He had a gaping space between his two front teeth that made him sound as though he was whistling when he talked. I thought I smelled cow manure on his boots when he walked over and put his arm around her shoulders, pulled her close, and tried to kiss her on the cheek. She pushed him away, laughing.

"Stop it, Cooter, I ain't in no mood for any more of your shenanigans."

"Well, I heerd you let Earl diddle you on the hay-ride last year. Ain't I good enough for you?"

"Stop them lies, Cooter!" Colleen yelled as she pushed him away. "You can't believe everything you hear in the barn. Now get away from me, you dumb-ass redneck."

With that, Cooter slinked back to his buddies and the other two girls who were falling over laughing at him. Colleen then put a few coins in the juke box. I got brave and walked over to where she was standing checking out the latest Elvis tunes. "I see you like Elvis too," I whispered. "You know, he shouldn't have talked to you that way, Miss."

She looked up at me with her sparkling, emerald eyes and quietly said, "He's just a harmless farm boy. I have to put him in his place at times. These guys are always feeding him stuff because he's so gullible."

"Well, it still isn't right," I replied.

"Don't worry," she responded, "I can handle them."

"Colleen is a very pretty name," I blurted.

"Thanks, I'm Irish."

"I'm Irish too!" I happily replied. "My name is Herbie."

"Nice to meet you, Herbie," Colleen smiled back with a flirting gleam in her eye.

Now I was hooked. "Do you come here often?" I stuttered. "I'm staying at my sister's camp on the other side of the lake for a week."

"I come once in a while on the weekend to go swimming and dancing."

"I love swimming and dancing. Will you be at the beach tomorrow? Maybe we can talk some more if you come." I was so excited that this beautiful girl talked to me that I just kept on rambling.

"I'm not sure," she smiled back.

"Well, I'll be here around noon and will look for you, if you don't mind."

"Sure," she replied just as a couple of the farm boys meandered over to see what was going on.

Seeing their hackles up, I decided it was best to leave before I got into trouble. These country bumpkins were a lot bigger than me. "Nice to meet you, Colleen. Hope to see you tomorrow," I whispered before they got any closer.

I quickly left just as the farm boys began hovering over Colleen and giving her the third degree about what we were talking about. "It was nothing," I heard her yell as I quickly headed back toward camp.

"How was the clubhouse?" Kathleen asked when I got back to the now roaring campfire.

"It was ok. There were a bunch of local yokels goofing on some pretty girl there."

"Oh, really," Steve smirked as I sat down in one of the lawn chairs near the fire pit.

"Goofing on her, hum, what does that mean, Herbie?" Steve continued to tease.

"Well, you know what I mean Steve, teasing her and saying stupid things."

"What kind of stupid things, Herbie?" Steve implored.

I was beginning to feel like I was in the Spanish inquisition and really didn't want to tell him what they said to her. Sensing I was getting uncomfortable with the conversation, Kathleen turned to Steve, who had a few cold beers under his belt after dinner, and told him to stop badgering me. She then remarked to me coyly, "I bet she was pretty, Herbie. Did you talk with her?"

"Just for a couple minutes because all those farmer kids saw me talking and started walking toward us. I got a little nervous and left. I didn't want to cause trouble. But she told me she might be at the beach tomorrow with her mom."

"Well, that's good. Maybe you can talk with her then."

"Maybe," I nonchalantly replied. Luckily, Suzie and Wendy emerged from the cabin with a bag of marshmallows and graham crackers, begging to make s'mores. That ended my inquisition as the discussion turned to whether they deserved to have s'mores because of all the whining Kathleen had to endure while I was at the pavilion.

After smacking a dozen mosquitos while sitting by the campfire toasting marshmallows, I decided to head to bed and dream about this beautiful, blond stranger I had just met. I fell right to sleep that night. However, I didn't dream of her. Instead, I had a dream about being trapped inside a smelly barn surrounded by a group of pitchfork-wielding farm boys. Luckily, I woke up because I had to pee. But instead of heading down to the stinky, wooden outhouse, I decided to go behind a pine tree in the back of our cabin.

I quickly fell back to sleep and didn't wake up again until I smelled bacon cooking and kids arguing again over something dumb. After a leisurely breakfast, I decided that I would be adventurous and swim the length of this small lake to the pavilion. I figured it would take about ten or fifteen minutes and that Colleen would be impressed when she saw me coming ashore looking like Buster Crab, without all the muscles, of course.

The pavilion didn't appear to be that far away when I entered the water around 11:30 that morning, but distances can be deceiving. I had a false sense of confidence because I had passed all my swimming tests in school this year, especially swimming laps, and figured this would be a piece of cake for me. Boy, was I wrong! I didn't take into consideration that it was extremely hot out, with a brutal sun and no clouds in the sky. The ten-minute swim I envisioned turned out to be a forty-five minute life-or-death ordeal. About half way across the lake, I began to feel exhausted and was dehydrated as I struggled to shore. Luckily, I had learned how to float in swimming class. Being able to float and preserve energy between strokes allowed me to survive, barely. Instead of walking gallantly out of the water like I planned, I ended up crawling ashore on my hands and knees gasping for air, bedraggled and red as a lobster. To add insult to injury, I saw Colleen waving furiously and smiling as she got into her mom's car, leaving me behind like pile of wet seaweed on the beach.

When I got back to camp, Kathleen looked at me and said, "Herbie, you have a wicked sunburn. Didn't you put sun tan lotion on?"

"No, I forgot."

"Boy, you're going to suffer tonight."

"Why?" I asked. "It doesn't feel bad now."

"Well, believe me, Herbie, it will later. So, what did your friend have to say?"

"I didn't get a chance to talk to her," I said dejectedly. "By the time I got to the beach, she was leaving with her mom. She just waved to me."

"That's too bad, Herbie; maybe she'll be back again during the week."

"I hope so."

After a dinner of hamburgers, hot dogs, potato salad, chips, pickles and watermelon, Steve announced that we were all going to the Riverview Drive-in about four miles away near the town of Stillwater. They had just re-released the 1951 horror movie classic "The Thing from Another World" starring James Arness and it was playing there. I still remember being scared to death as a seven year old when Dorothy and her new boyfriend Art Hilt took me to see it the first time at the Hollywood Drive-in near Troy. But as a teenager, I now relished watching horror movies. (It must be an adolescent thing.)

Although it was pretty warm out that night sitting on the hood of Steve's car watching the movie and munching on pop-corn, I was starting to get chilled and didn't feel well. When we got back to the camp, I was really feeling bad and couldn't stop shivering.

Kathleen put her hand on my forehead and said I had a fever. She gave me a big glass of water and a couple aspirins and told me I was dehydrated from all that sun. She then had me take my tee shirt off and rubbed some cocoa butter on my back and chest and told me to go to bed.

What a horrible night I had, shivering and delirious. Scenes of flaming monsters were interspersed with visions of a beautiful blond angel with a ponytail and hazel eyes, smiling and telling me everything was going to be ok. The soft hand on my forehead and soothing words all through the night was Kathleen checking on me.

Around daybreak my fever broke and I awoke, with my bed clothes drenched in perspiration. Kathleen told me I had been talking crazy in my sleep all night and that I was burning up. "It looks like your fever finally broke, Herbie. Do you feel any better?"

"A little weak and thirsty," I replied meekly, "but better."

"I hope you learned your lesson, Herbie," Kathleen said as she handed me a big glass of orange juice. "Drink this," she insisted. "I'll have some pancakes and sausage ready in a few minutes." She then turned her attention to Wendy and Susie and told them to stop whining over who was going to stir the pancake batter. "Stop it you two, now!" Those girls reminded me so much of my sisters Brenda and Jan arguing over who was going to get to lick the chocolate frosting off the wooden spoon used to make a birthday cake.

Every day during the rest of my stay I meandered over to the pavilion in hopes that Colleen would be there. Friday night was especially nerve wracking because I knew she loved to dance. Sadly, she never returned, but that beautiful vision of her remained in my subconscious. You never know...maybe she'd turn up later in my life. I could only hope. So the week came to an end, most of my sunburn had peeled away, and I headed home from an adventure I'd never forget.

CHAPTER TWENTY-EIGHT

Cruising!

During my junior and senior years I began questioning the long term friendships I had with my close school buddies. I guess it might have been emotional as well as physical growing pains. I'm not sure, but definite changes were occurring that I don't think any of us realized at the time. I think Bill and Larry were beginning to distance me for whatever reason.

Ronnie got his driver's license in the spring of our junior year. It was lucky for us that his dad let him use the family car to go to his part time job downtown stocking shelves at Cahill's Sporting Goods. So, of course, Larry, Billy and I immediately took advantage of Ronnie, conning him into letting us cruise around town in his dad's car with him after work. Boy, did we feel like hotshots hanging out the back window hooting and hollering at the girls. You see, Friday night was cruising night for Troy teenagers. On any given Friday night you'd see dozens of guys parading their shiny vehicles up and down River and Third Streets, each trying to out-do the other in an attempt to garner attention and impress the hotties waiting to get into Paul's or the Mayflower or maybe even enticing some to hop in the back seat for a joyride around town. Who knows, some of the girls might give up a cheap feel for the thrill of riding in some grease monkey's souped-up hotrod.

For a few weeks we were able to get away with our little con job. That was until one Friday night when Ronnie's sister Velma saw us cruising around town and begged to hop in the back seat and ride around with us. But when Ronnie refused, she swore she'd get revenge, which she did by squealing on Ronnie to her father. She whined that she had to take the bus home because Ronnie refused to drive her even though he knew she was sick. Then she carped about him always being too busy because he was cruising around town with us and trying to pick up girls. Needless to say, all hell broke loose when Ronnie got home. He was grounded from driving to work for a month and our exciting cruising excursions came to an abrupt end. We were relegated to hoofing it again. Ironically, the only girl willing to ride with us during that entire three-week stint was, you guessed it: Velma.

Back in the 1950s and early 60s, being able to customize a car, re-build a motor, or change your own spark plugs, brakes or oil was commonplace. Not like today. Today when you lift up the hood of a car, it's like peering into a jet engine with all the high tech do-dads and stuff. Back then we didn't have all the Jiffy Lubes, Midas Mufflers or Firestones to get cars serviced. Instead, if you had car trouble, you either fixed it yourself or went to a local garage to have work done.

Ironically, I had a short-lived job during the summer of my sophomore year as a grease monkey and attendant at Pearlman's Gas Station on River Street, thanks to Tony Fermetti. Tony was a regular customer and good friend of the owner and put in a good word for me. Big mistake on Tony's part because I was totally inept at anything mechanical and scared to death to work there. But I was desperate to earn some money because my hours at the car wash down at the Hendrick Hudson Garage had been cut back. The closest I ever came to working on a car was when I handed Gene Koch a wrench as he was putting in a set of brakes in one of his beat-up jalopies. I was totally insecure about my mechanical skills.

I almost failed basic shop in grade school. I was so inept that I didn't know the difference between a dipstick and a dipshit. After a week of working at Pearlman's, I did figure out what a dipstick was but it took me a couple weeks longer to realize I was pretty much a dipshit. I was afflicted with *Murphy's Law*—"If anything can go wrong, it will." In my case it went something like this: "If you think you're going to screw up and fail, you will," and I did.

Pearlman's was a good two miles from my house, so to save money on bus fare I would walk to and from work every day. Boy, was that tough. I think that summer was the hottest in the history of mankind. By the time I got to work I was drenched in sweat and by the end of my shift, I could ring out my grease-stained tee shirt with enough perspiration to fill an empty oil can. I came home each night grimy, smelly and exhausted. Why did work have to be so hard?

Jake the owner seemed like a real nice guy the day I started. He brought me into the office and told me what I'd be doing. To start, I would work in the back room filling up oil cans when a customer wanted the cheaper, recycled oil that he kept in a fifty-gallon drum. He also had shelves of the more expensive canned oil in the back room, as well as in racks near the island that housed the gasoline pumps. I followed him around like a puppy dog the first couple days clutching a rag in my hand at all times and keeping an extra one in the back pocket of my dungarees. Jake told me that the customer was always right, even if he acted like a peckerhead. Customers were real nice most of the time, especially if everything went smoothly, and they usually did when Jake was taking care of them.

A shiny, white, 1959 Buick Electra 225 convertible, with its sweeping fins and red leather seats, soon glided into a spot next to the high test pump. Seated in this babe mobile was a dapper, gray-haired man in his late fifty's. Beside him sat a gorgeous, blue-eyed blond who appeared to be half his age, wearing a pink cotton blouse and a polka dot scarf around her neck. She had her legs crossed exposing her svelte thighs nestled under her light blue skirt.

"Wow," I thought to myself, "this job is going to be great!"

The driver peered at me standing behind Jake and quipped, "Looks like you hired another deserving Troylet to help you out. They don't seem to last too long do they, Jake?"

"Well I've had a tough time keeping help this year, Carl. I am hoping Herbie here will fill the bill," Jake replied, looking over his shoulder at me. That statement made me feel pretty good at the time. But things would change rapidly. "So what do you need today, Carl?" Jake asked.

"Fill her up with high test and check the oil. We're going to Bennington for the weekend and don't want to run out of oil again like a couple weeks ago. I think I've got a leak down there somewhere."

"Well, when you get back, bring her in and I'll check it out for you. It might be just a bad gasket."

"Ok, I will."

Jake then removed the hose from the gas pump, inserted it into the tank and secured a latch in the handle so the pump would continue to work. This allowed Jake time to walk to the front of the car where he pried open the hood. "Watch this, Herbie," Jake said, as he pulled out a long thin rod from the engine. He took his rag and wiped off the end. "Herbie, this is how you check the oil. Do you see these lines?" Jake asked, pointing to a section of the dip-stick with cross-hatched markings. "When I put this back in and pull it out, if the oil isn't between these two marks, he needs a quart of oil."

"Oh, ok," I replied, not exactly understanding.

"Carl, you're down a quart," Jake said, walking to the driver and showing him the dipstick. " You want a quart of the good stuff?"

"Nah, if it's going to continue to leak until I get it fixed, I'd be throwing good money after bad, and I hate wasting money."

"I know you do, you old tight wad!" Jake laughed.

"You know me too well," Carl laughed back. "Give me the cheap shit you're hiding in the back."

"Herbie, take this can and fill it up to the line near the top."

"Ok," I said warily as I raced back into the garage. This was the first time I ever used the oil pump by myself. My hands were shaking as I held the can under the nozzle and began cranking the handle. Within seconds a stream of black, smelly crude oozed into the can. I didn't want to screw this up, but as luck would have it I overflowed the can before I could stop, and a puddle of "Beverly Hills crude" was now simmering on the hot concrete floor. "Oh shit," I thought. I better wipe this up before Jake comes back here. By the time I got out with the can of oil, I could hear Carl complaining about what was taking me so long. As I handed the can to Jake, he noticed how full it was and told me to be more careful and not to fill it over the line. I shook my head then watched as he poured the oil. Even with his steady hand a little excess oil splattered onto the red hot manifold creating an immediate stench. Needless to say, Carl wasn't a happy camper and kvetched to Jake about my ineptness.

"Sorry, Carl, I won't charge you for the oil. Ok?"

"Yea, it's ok this time. But if it happens again, you won't see me back here."

"It won't happen again," Jake grimaced as he turned and glared at me.

Amazingly, I lasted three weeks, but they were three weeks from hell for poor Jake. He tried his best to tolerate all my stupid mistakes: overfilling gas tanks and spilling gas on the ground; undercharging customers because I pumped more gas than they wanted because I was too busy checking their oil; knocking off a wiper blade when washing one guy's windshield; not giving correct change to customers and them screaming at me and Jake because of my stupidity.

When I came to work that last Friday, Jake was standing at the office door with an envelope in his hand. Behind him I could see a kid about my age standing there with a grin on his face. Jake handed me the envelope containing my last week's pay, twenty dollars, and said, "I'm sorry, Herbie, but I have to let you go. You're a good kid but you're not cut out for this kind of work." My heart sank because this was the first time I got fired. I felt like a failure. But I knew in my heart Jake was right, I wasn't cut out for that kind of work. With a heavy heart and a hangdog expression, I thanked Jake for giving me a try then slowly walked away, glancing over my shoulder as Jake put his hand on my replacement's shoulder and walked him into the garage. The hardest part of losing my job was hearing from Tony that I blew my opportunity.

CHAPTER TWENTY-NINE

At the Car Wash

Luckily, I was able to get more hours at the car wash with my brother-in-law, Andy. That job continued to be an interesting adventure for me. I came in earlier than Andy, usually right after school. He worked full time during the day at Troy District Shirt Company in Cohoes but came down to the car wash after supper and on Saturdays. Most of our money came from tips which we were supposed to share. It seemed strange to me that Andy always ended up with more than me for some reason. In the beginning I could understand because Andy was much faster than me. He washed more cars and had to drive the finished cars to and from their parking spots. But as time went by, though I became very proficient myself, the tips never increased. Since I didn't have a license to drive the cars like Andy did, I just let it slide. However, I really wanted to try my hand at parking them.

Andy was understandably reluctant to let me drive any cars because he didn't want to risk losing his part time job if I screwed up. But when he found out kids on the early shift were doing just that, he decided to let me try. Boy, that turned out to be an adventure.

The garage had four indoor parking levels and an outside lot on the river bank next to the garage. When an order came in from the gate house where patrons registered to have their cars washed, the car keys were stapled to the order and a number code showed its location. Those keys were then kept on a board just inside the car wash. "Herbie, here is your chance. When you finish the car you're working on, back it out and leave it by the wall. When I finish this car, I will park them both upstairs."

"Great," I replied breathlessly. "I'll be done in a minute, Andy." Rushing to finish, I hopped into the driver's seat and quickly started the engine. I could barely reach the brake and gas pedal and had to move the seat all the way up because my legs were so short. That's when I remembered all the important things Tony Fermetti taught me years earlier when he gave me driving lessons at Saint Mary's Cemetery (especially the time I almost drove his car into a ravine). Remembering them now gave me a false sense of security, so when I put the car in reverse it lurched backward and shuddered to an abrupt stop as I slammed on the brakes. Seeing a huge, concrete support beam rapidly approaching in the rear view mirror had sent me into a state of panic, causing me to stall the engine.

"What the hell was that?" Andy yelled when he heard the brakes screech.

"It's nothing," I yelled back, not wanting to tell him I almost hit the post. I quickly got out of the car and went into the bathroom until I could stop trembling. I didn't want Andy to see I was scared shitless over what happened. When I came out, Andy had already parked the car upstairs and had brought in two more cars to be washed. For some strange reason, he never said another word about the incident that day.

However, I had a few other incidents I didn't tell Andy about. Like the time I came in early and there was a silver Cadillac parked next to the wall with the keys in it. The kid who washed it was supposed to drive it to the upper level and park it. However, he didn't. Instead he just punched out figuring someone else would finish the job for him. Of course, with no one around but me and me now filled with confidence because I had parked a few recently without further incidence, I decided it would be a piece of cake to drive this boat upstairs. That's when it got interesting.

I had no problem driving to the upper deck. With no space open to just pull the car in, I was forced to back into a narrow space next to a concrete support column. I looked in the rear view mirror and slowly backed up, but suddenly I heard a horrible scraping sound. "Oh shit!" I thought to myself. "I hope that wasn't me." I warily walked around to the side next to the post and almost had a heart attack. That shiny, newly-washed Cadillac now had a six-inch gash along the passenger side door. Panicked I thought, "What the hell am I going to do now? I'm screwed if they find out."

Fearing I'd get fired, my mind raced back to the time I broke Eddie Barrow's bike. "Hmmm," I thought, "nobody saw me come in; the kid who was supposed to park it left; I was trying to do him a favor and there was a slight, minor scratch. So, if I go back down and no one is around yet, who is to know, right?"

There was no one around when I punched in, so I waited at the punch clock near the gate house for a few minutes with my card in my hand. Luckily, Charlie the gate house attendant came strolling around the corner with a coffee in his hand. "How are you doing, Herbie?"

"I'm...good, Charlie." I said, stammering. "I just punched in. Anything new?"

"Nothing, it's been pretty quiet."

"Well, that's good," I said, as a blue Pontiac pulled up to the gate. With a sigh of relief I was soon washing that Pontiac with a vengeance, hoping that no one would find out about my Cadillac debacle. Just then Andy walked in with a handful of tickets for several more cars to wash. It turned out to be a very busy, stressful night and no one got fired. I guess the owner never noticed the scratch when he picked up his car, and when he did see it, he must have figured it got hit while he was at one of those ritzy, newfangled shopping centers in Latham.

When we got done working that night, it was still fairly early, around 7:30. Instead of going right home after work, we decided to play some pool over at Whitey's pool hall. With a couple bucks in change from tips in my pocket and an additional four dollars I kept in the beat- up wallet I made at the Boys Club years earlier, we headed upstairs to shoot a rack of pool. The loser would pay the winner fifty cents.

I had never played pool with Andy before, so I didn't know what to expect. I figured he'd be a pushover. I'd been playing quite a bit lately with Larry and thought I was pretty good at straight pool. Eight ball and nine ball, not so much, they were hustlers' games. I thought that to win those games you had to be extremely lucky or cheat. In straight pool you just had to be good. As luck would have it, I started off great. I was leading Andy eighteen to nine in a game of rack twenty five. I had just run off seven shots in a row before missing. That was when the tables turned. I hopped up onto the high-backed stool to watch, anticipating Andy might run off three or four shots before missing then I'd finish him off with a flurry. However, to my chagrin, he kept sinking shot after shot. Soon I began sensing he was going to beat me, and, being a sore loser, I started whining that he was just a lucky, redneck Canuck.

Instead of those remarks bothering Andy, they just made him laugh as he continued to sink shot after shot after shot. When the game ended, I picked up the quarters and angrily threw them at Andy who was still laughing. I vowed I would whip his ass the next game. By the end of the night I was still fuming having lost every single game and called Andy every expletive I could think of as he pocketed all my tip money. I didn't say another word to him when he drove me home that night. I later found out that he and his brother Desmond were notorious pool hustlers up in their home town. Anita Sueii had been their neighbor in Canada and told me all about it when she moved into Denny Barrow's old house the next summer. Had I met her before, I never would have played Andy for money knowing he was a hustler.

CHAPTER THIRTY

For Christmas Sake

Andy and I continued to work at the car wash without much drama until the Christmas holiday. I came to work right after school the Friday before Christmas and immediately started working. Several cars were backed up waiting to be done and Charlie the gatehouse attendant was complaining about it. It seems everyone was celebrating the holidays early with work parties and last minute shopping downtown. The city was really bustling, with Salvation Army volunteers ringing their bells and holiday music filling the air. Grumpy Jack Doyle, a burly cop with decades on the job, was vigorously directing traffic at the intersection of River, Fulton and Third Street in his usual animated way, blowing his whistle and waving to smiling shoppers as they rushed across the crowded streets.

Andy finally showed up around five-thirty with a shit-eating grin on his puss. The reason I say he had a shit-eating grin is because he was shit-faced. He was carrying a large plastic shopping bag containing a half empty bottle of Jack Daniels, a bottle of Seven-Up and a soggy, half filled, plastic bag containing ice cubes and plastic cups. He stumbled off the curb as he entered the car wash and was soon mumbling a Christmas greeting to me and Charlie.

I knew he was in trouble the minute he opened his mouth and slurred his words. It was difficult enough dealing with his Canadian accent when he was sober, but now I needed an interpreter to understand him. Hanging up his coat, he plopped himself on a chair at our break table near the overhead hot air heater. He then poured himself a seven' n seven and another for me. "Ca'mon, Herdie, ha, a dlink wid me."

"No thanks, Andy. Looks like you've had a few too many already."

"Na, em fynne, ok? I can hole my lickr, doan u wurry."

"Yeah right, you crazy Canuck," I said. Cliff always said Indians and fire water don't mix. Now I know what he meant.

"Thas bullchit! I can hole my lickr, doan you wurry, doan you wurry," he yelled as he headed to the bathroom.

It was close to seven-thirty when I finished my last car. I was in a hurry to head over to see Larry at EJ Shoes and then stop by and see Billy at his busboy job at Woolworths. I figured Andy was probably sobering up by this time. I hadn't noticed him drinking any more in the last hour or so and figured he was ok. I grabbed my coat and a big handful of coins from the tip jar as I was leaving, handed in my slip to Charlie at the gate to get my night's pay, punched out and went to see Larry. As luck would have it, Larry had left early that night so I headed over to Woolworths to check on Billy. He had been working his new job there since the fall.

The lunch counter was crowded with shoppers, but there was one lone stool at the end of the counter next to the kitchen. I quickly sat down and ordered a grilled cheese sandwich and a Coke. My waitress was a pleasant older woman, around forty, with dishwater blond hair pulled back into a neat bun. Thin strands of silver highlighting her hair made it appear as though she had it styled at an expensive beauty salon, instead of from a bottle of Toni hair coloring and Dippity-Do.

"Ma'am, is Billy working tonight? I asked after placing my order.

"He's in the back. Let me get him"

"Thanks." In a couple minutes Billy came out wiping his brow. His white apron was covered with grease, mustard and ketchup stains. His right hand sported a large gauze bandage and wooden splint on this middle finger. 'What the hell happened to you, Billy? Do you always give your customers the finger?"

"Not funny, dick-head. I just got back from the hospital because I broke a friggin glass emptying the dishwasher."

"Yuk," I replied.

"They put in three stiches and gave me a tetanus shot. The shot hurt worse than getting cut."

"Poor baby..."

"Up yours," he responded, giving me the finger.

"Only kidding, Billy," I said. "Looks like you won't be bowling for a while."

"Nah, the doctor said it should be fine in a week or two."

"Well, I guess you won't be going out tonight then."

"Not tonight, for sure. But call me tomorrow. Maybe we can all go to the movies or something."

"Ok," I replied. "I guess I'll head home then—I'm kind of pooped anyway—I washed a ton of cars tonight. Hey before I forget, you should've seen my crazy ass brother-in-law today. He was plastered.

"How come?" asked Billy.

"Too much partying at work, I guess. I never saw him drunk before, but he was so funny."

"I always liked Andy," Billy said. "How is he getting home?"

"I don't know. I guess he'll probably drive himself home. He drove to work drunk without a problem."

"I hope you're right," Billy said.

"I'm pretty sure he's ok by now. I didn't see him drink anything for a couple hours." With that I finished my sandwich and Billy headed back into the kitchen.

It was around quarter of ten by the time I walked home. A beleaguered Patty was at the door and yelled, "Where the hell's Andy?"

Stunned, I replied, "I don't know. He was still washing cars when I left, around seven- thirty. Why?"

"He was supposed to be home early tonight and I haven't heard a thing from him. Why didn't you wait for him to take you home? Was he drunk? I know they had a party at work today."

"Well...He did act a bit strange when he first came in but seemed ok when I left," I replied, not wanting to scare her or bag him. "He was still washing cars and waved to me when I left. I told him I was meeting Larry and Billy and didn't need a ride."

"Well, I called down there at nine o'clock and no one answered. Now I'm really worried," she sighed with tears welling up in her red eyes.

"If you're worried, Patty, I'll run back down and look for him."

"No, no Herbie, that'll take too long." Luckily, Dorothy and Jimmy had come to visit Ma that night and were having coffee in the kitchen when Patty rushed through the door in a panic. "Jimmy, can you take Herbie down to check on Andy, please?" Patty begged. "I'm worried sick something happened to him. He's never this late."

Glancing over at Dorothy for approval, Jimmy immediately agreed then said to me, "Ok, Herbie, let's go." Within a few minutes Jimmy guided his big, black, Buick sedan with its two suicide knobs on the steering wheel into the darkened entrance to the parking garage. It was eerily quiet with all the lights out in the building as Jimmy grumbled to me. "Boy, this doesn't look good, Herbie,"

Spotting Andy's car parked by the entrance ramp, we approached it and found it empty, with no sign of Andy. Jimmy raced back to his car, grabbed a flashlight from the glove compartment and warily pointed the light into the car washing stall. When he saw nothing, he declared, "Herbie, we better go up the ramp, maybe he fell or something up there."

"Ok, Jimmy," I replied—now scared half to death that Andy was injured or maybe even dead. Pangs of guilt permeated my mind. "I should have stayed with him instead of leaving him like

I did." Just as we turned to walk up the ramp, I noticed a sliver of light under the bathroom door. "Hey, Jimmy there's a light under the door. Maybe it's him," I whispered, hoping it was but fearing the worst. Quickly we walked over to the door listening to hear if someone was in there. After a few moments we heard a recurring sound similar to a small motor sputtering.

Jimmy then knocked on the door and asked, "Is anyone there? Is anyone there?" After several more requests and no answer, Jimmy grabbed the door knob and yanked it open. Immediately, a brilliant light permeated the hallway. What we saw was shocking: Andy with his pants down around his ankles, snoring to beat the band, passed out cold on the throne. If only we had a camera.

Needless to say, as scary as it was at the time, we knew Andy would have hell to pay the next day when he sobered up. But we also knew we could replay this story over and over again for years to come, all the while laughing our asses off at Andy's expense.

CHAPTER THIRTY-ONE

Well, Hello...Dotty!

Billy's finger healed in record time and he was soon his old self. Billy was very frugal and saved a lot of money in order to buy the car he was always bragging about. For some reason, Billy was enthralled by the Chevy Corvair, first released by General Motors in 1960. He had his eye on a used tan convertible being worked on by Hank Marcy in auto-mechanics class. Hank was recognized as the best mechanic in our school.

It took Hank most of the winter of our junior year to rebuild the engine and complete the body work. Ironically, the guy who originally owned the car had donated it to the school to be sold to the highest bidder that summer. When it went on sale, Billy was able to snatch it up for six hundred bucks—a steal. Although it exhausted most of Billy's savings, it offered him an opportunity to join the elite of our class: Car owner.

It was around 11:00 am when Billy called. "Wake up, Herbie, wake up," Ma yelled, poking me out of my erotic dream. "Billy's on the phone."

Still groggy, I picked up the phone and answered gruffly. "What's up, Billy? What's so important this early in the morning?"

"You dipshit, it's after eleven. Get your ass out of bed and get moving, I'll pick you up in fifteen minutes."

Shocked, I replied, "you got the car?"

"Yep and we're going for a joy ride. So get moving." Soon Billy, Larry and I were cruising around town with Billy and Larry in the front seat and me relegated to the back seat. With the convertible top down we enjoyed the warm summer breeze. But with the wind whistling past my ears and the air-cooled engine in the back making a racket, I could barely hear Billy bragging to Larry about how great his new buggy was.

"I can get this baby up to sixty in about six seconds,"

"Prove it, hotshot," Larry taunted as we left Prospect Park and our grand tour around the pool and tennis courts.

"Ok, dick-head, I'll prove it," Billy shot back, taking the bait. We were soon on Oakwood Ave and the thrill ride began. "Ok, now I'll show you what this baby's got under the hood," Billy bellowed as he floored it in front of Oakwood Cemetery. Within seconds, we were thrown backwards as this little puddle jumper lurched forward. The more speed we picked up, the louder the engine screeched in my ear.

"Holy shit, Billy! Slow down!" Larry pleaded as this little beast accelerated faster and faster. I said nothing. Instead I just prayed and held onto the back seat for dear life. The more Larry whined, the faster Billy went until he saw the flashing lights about a quarter mile ahead. Quickly he hit the brakes and began to slow. Luckily, the Troy cops had just pulled over another speeder ahead of us, otherwise Billy would have gotten his first speeding ticket. Breathing a sigh of relief, Larry told Billy to make a quick stop at Tom's snack bar which was coming up quickly on our right.

"Why should I?" Billy shot back.

"We got to stop there, Billy. I hear they got a new babe working there."

"Who told you that crap, Beresny?"

"Yea, he was here last week and said he couldn't stop drooling."

"Ok, let's check her out," Billy said, quickly pulling into the half-filled parking lot.

Within a few minutes a beautiful, buxom babe with a low cut blouse, short shorts, bobby sox and pink sneakers was hovering over our car. "Hi, fellas, how can I help yah?" she said. Her blue eyes twinkled enticingly as she leaned over checking out the car while we were checking out her boobs. Within seconds all three of us were drooling. That's when Larry, the bullshit artist, began his thing.

"How long you been working here, gorgeous?" Larry asked.

"About two weeks now," she replied, blushing slightly.

"So what's your name?

"Dottie Merle. What's yours?"

"Dottie Merle," Larry repeated. "What a lovely name. I'm Larry, that's Billy," he said, pointing at Billy who had a wide smile on his face. "Oh, yeah, and that's Herbie in the back," he said, as an afterthought. "You're so beautiful you could be the next Miss America, right guys?" Larry said, poking Billy and glancing back at me.

"Oh yeah, she sure could," Billy said, as I nodded my approval.

Now totally flummoxed and in full blush, Dottie proceeded to take our order: Three cheeseburgers, fries, two Cokes and one vanilla shake. After she headed back to the snack bar to hand in our order, we continued to ogle her. "Holy shit, Larry, you're right. She's so...hot. Beresny finally got one right."

"I told you so," Larry said, "Maybe we can take her for a joy ride after she gets off work. What do you think, Billy?"

"No way, I'm taking Rose to the drive-in tonight."

"Maybe we can double date if I can talk her into it. What do you think?"

"Maybe," Billy replied as I slumped quietly in the back seat feeling left out. I had been starting to feel slightly estranged from my buddies for the past year or so but always just brushed it off.

A few minutes later Dottie sashayed back with our order. Assuring us he could get us a better view of Dottie's endowments, Larry connived to accidently drop our money onto his lap when he went to pay. However, when he did, it took Dottie by surprise. In the blink of an eye, the tray she was holding slipped out of her hand and was now partially tilted on Larry's lap. Most of our order landed on him and Billy's new floor mats. "Oh shit, oh shit, they're hot," Larry whined, as he brushed off an of order fries onto Billy's new floor mats. Soon his vanilla shake was dripping off his brand new khaki shorts into a puddle on the floor, as Billy reached over to save the cheeseburgers before they plummeted as well.

Dottie began to whimper, "I am so sorry, it was an accident."

That's when a rough looking guy in a cowboy hat with a cigar hanging out of his mouth came over to check on Dottie. "What happened, Dottie?" her boyfriend Alan asked.

"I accidently dropped their order, Alan. I feel awful," she said, as tears raced down her cheeks.

Billy was quietly pissing and moaning to Larry about how his car was wrecked and that Larry was going pay to get it cleaned, and Larry was busily picking up the remnants of our fries from the floor. "You and your dumb ideas" Billy mumbled. He was totally pissed but could do little now because Dottie's boyfriend was there and he didn't need to get in an argument with him too. The whole time I just sat in the back, smirking to myself and taking it all in. I didn't need to do or say anything.

Luckily, Alan told us that he would pay for our order. He then put his arm around Dottie and walked away. We gobbled down what we could salvage then headed over to Hoffman's Car Wash in Latham to get Billy's car cleaned. Larry coughed up the $2.50 charge.

That was the one and only time I remember riding in Billy's new car. However, he and Larry drove to Lake George several times that summer with Rose and Sue. I don't ever remember being invited on any of their excursions. I was slowly beginning to realize that things were changing.

CHAPTER THIRTY-TWO

There Once Was an Indian Maid

Anita was a young Abernaki woman who came to live with her cousin Jillian Joubett's family in Denny Barrow's old house. She was several years older than me and most guys on the street. However, her age didn't stop the older guys from hitting on her when she'd hang out at Margie's Grill on upper Congress Street on the weekends. She was quite tall, brown-skinned and had shoulder length black hair. She didn't fit the mold of the beautiful Indian maiden. Her face had more of a rugged frontier look with small pockmarks caused by a severe case of chicken pox as a child. Although she wasn't what you would call pretty, she had a simmering sexuality about her that would trigger a rush of testosterone in most guys.

Coincidentally, it was that spring and summer when Billy, Larry and I began hanging out Margie's because we could get served there without a problem. They never checked us for proof of age because we were befriended by Louie Staley, the bartender who loved to bullshit with us. We soon became regulars. He was one of the most affable bartenders in town and eventually tended bar for my brother Frank when he opened the Spring Lounge. Louie was an old-time Ida Hiller who privately held the same distain we held for the snooty RPI kids who occasionally frequented the place when they felt like slumming. Usually, they indulged their licentious behavior at frat parties.

Although I had been introduced to Anita previously by Andy, I didn't really get to know her until I ran into her at Margie's.

Occasionally I'd walk home with her after Professor Tossi finished playing his gig around midnight on Friday and Saturday nights. Prof Tossi, as he was affectionately known, played piano and sang mostly old standards on a small stage located in the back of the bar. He took requests and encouraged everyone to sing along with him. Larry and I often volunteered to go on stage and sing duets. If Billy was with us and in the mood, then the three of us would sing. We all loved folk music and the Kingston Trio in particular and favorites like "Charlie and the MTA" and "Tom Dooley." As hard as we tried, we could never get Anita to come up and sing with us. But she loved to tell jokes and tease Larry and me about our singing or comment how awful Prof Tossi sang. He *definitely* wasn't a crooner.

I walked Anita home from Margie's for several weekends and thought I was beginning to know her fairly well. But after listening to all the stories the older guys told about how easy she was, I stupidly started believing them, even though she never acted like that with me. But being a guy, I decided to give romance a shot and make my move. The problem was I never learned any moves, and if I had, I'd probably trip over them trying to use them.

I think I was developing a crush on Anita. So on a fateful Friday night I had a few beers under my belt and began to feel my courage rising as well as my hormone levels. It was now or never. Maybe she was attracted to me. She sure loved talking to me all those nights, I thought. Ironically, this was the same night my sister Jan was sleeping over at her friend Ellenor Kiljoy's house. (The Kiljoys lived on the first floor and the Joubetts on the second.) It was a little after midnight when we got to her front porch and Anita was on a roll joking about the two, drunk, RPI guys who tried to hit on her at Margie's until Louie threw them out. Just as she was finishing her story, she opened the front door, said she was bushed, and needed to go to bed.

As she walked into the darkened hall, I quickly followed her. My heart was racing because I was now in uncharted territory. Noticing that I was still there she turned to me and said, "Herbie, I had a lot of fun tonight, but you have to go home now, it's getting late."

"I know, I know, I'm sorry...I just thought...can I ask you a favor before I go?"

"What might that be, Herbie?" she responded with a sly undertone to her voice.

"Can I...please kiss you goodnight?"

Feigning shock Anita smiled through the darkness. "Herbie, I think you're a sweet kid, but I don't think that would be a good idea."

"Why?" I pleaded as my heart sank.

"Well, I'm at least five years older than you to start off with and I'm not really looking for romance at this point in my life," she said.

"But the guys..."

"Stop right there, Herbie," she insisted forcefully. "Don't believe all the bull guys like to throw around, ok?" Stunned I just stood there speechless—I felt like that idiot Cooter at Pine Lake. I had stepped over the line of our friendship. "Herbie, I'm not angry with you. I know you have all kinds of thoughts and desires. You're horny! I'm just not the one to satisfy your horniness, even though guys may have told you I would—I won't!"

Boy, did I really feel bad now and even more stupid than before. The first time I got up the nerve to even approach a girl about making out—I picked the wrong one. I could hear muffled giggling coming from the Killjoys' apartment. In the darkness I could see Anita with her finger pressed against her lips, shushing me to be silent and summarily waving me out the door. I limped home like a wounded puppy with his tail between his legs. My pride and my ego were shattered. I felt like a fool. I felt guilty. I felt horrible for even thinking of making out with Anita. It wasn't that I was just horny, I really liked her. I was smitten and she rejected me.

CHAPTER THIRTY-THREE

Margie the Drill Sargent

Even though I totally screwed up trying to hit on Anita, I still continued to go to Margie's with Larry and Billy and once in a while with Beresny. However, Anita wasn't there as much because she had begun hanging out with friends she'd met at a Watervliet bar. That became her new hangout. As I have well documented, we all had some ambivalence when it came RPI students. We liked some and despised others. For one, we liked Sach, a student who lived in Alan's house for a couple years because he was cool, had a Harley and a souped-up Chevy with mag wheels. We also liked the RPI hockey players we watched play at the field house and eventually drank with. We were also friendly with frat members who had let Larry and Billy into a few of their beer parties. Guys who hit on some girls we wanted at Margie's or guys who made jokes about us while we were singing or guys who just had arrogance about them when we tried to talk to them at the bar—we despised them.

Larry, Beresny and I had been hitting bars downtown and decided to finish the night at Margie's. I wasn't feeling too good after stuffing myself with crackers and cheese at the Troy bowl, peanuts at Dempsey's, and pickled kielbasi at Cooney's on Sixth Avenue. I had also mixed a couple glasses of Thunderbird (Beresny's favorite) with a few Genny Cream Ales. By the time we got to Margie's, my stomach was roiling. To make things even worse, a couple RPI guys sat down at the table next to us and started busting on Troy, Margie's and Prof Tossi, who was just finishing up his gig for the night. They were half in the bag but we were too wiped ourselves to confront them.

We were just finishing up our last beer when I really started to feel sick. I raced to the men's room. The main stairway to the rest-rooms split like a fork in the road about three steps up. The men's room then split to the left with five more stairs and the ladies' room split to the right. Half-way up the stairs, I purged covering the last two steps and splattering against the wall. Luckily, I was able get to the sink, wash my face and take a leak before anyone else came up. However, just as I was drying my hands, two RPI geeks came in gagging as I hustled back down the stairs, carefully avoiding my mess. Just as I reached the split in the staircase, I ran into Margie heading to the ladies' room.

"Hi, Margie," I said.

"Hi," she replied. But as I started to walk away she noticed the mess. She yelled at me, "Who the hell did that?"

I just shrugged my shoulders like I didn't know and played dumb, then said to her, "I think a couple guys are up there now. Maybe they know." I quickly raced back to our table as Margie marched up the stairs with fire in her eyes. "Come on, you guys. Let's get out of here quick!" I whispered to Larry and Beresny.

"Why, what's the matter?" Larry asked.

"I'll tell you when we get out of here. Now move!" The three of us were at the front door when all hell broke loose. Margie was screaming at the top of her lungs about those guys making my mess and them pleading to her that they didn't. When we were safely down by Lilly's, I told them what happened. They laughed and said in unison: "Couldn't happen to a nicer couple of guys." With that we headed home for the night. It was something like poetic justice!

CHAPTER THIRTY-FOUR

Colonial/Hockey/Frat Parties

On the way home from work one night, Larry came across a bar near Cluett's called the Colonial Tavern. It would become one of his favorite hangouts, along with Callahan's Tavern on the corner of Eighth and Hoosick Streets—a block from his house. What was so interesting about the Colonial was several RPI hockey players hung out there. Being newly indoctrinated hockey fans, we stopped by occasionally, play pool or just shoot the breeze with John Tracy, the owner, and some of the players who will remain nameless. They know who they are. Tracy, as he was affectionately called, was an affable guy and a father figure to several hockey players over the years. He also let them drink there which might not have set too well with their legendary coach Ned Harkness, a strict disciplinarian.

Even prior to meeting those players at Tracy's we'd been sneaking in to see RPI games at the field house using one of our time-honored techniques: one guy buys a student ticket for seventy-five cents, then surreptitiously pries open the back door so the rest of us can sneak in and run to unoccupied seats near the top of the arena.

Tracy's became a fairly regular hangout especially for Larry because it was on his way home from work. He and Billy bragged to me how they saw some of the "hockey groupies" dancing on the pool tables. They also hinted about guys making out in a dark corner of the bar on the nights John was off. How come I always seemed to miss out on all the good stuff? I wonder now if they made all that stuff up just to make me feel left out. Well it worked—I did feel left out.

I also missed out on most of the RPI frat parties Larry started attending because I wasn't asked. Plus I didn't know anything about where and when they were being held. The fraternities usually didn't let outsiders into their parties unless they knew you or you were a female, high school groupie. Larry apparently knew some of the members because he met them at his job or some bar. He was expanding his areas of interest much more than me while Billy was spending more time with his girlfriend Rose.

I did go to a one frat on Pawling Avenue with Larry late one Friday night but didn't like it. I didn't know anyone there but Larry did, plus all the girls were spoken for. A couple of the girls I recognized were classmates who had come with Troy High guys who were either invited or crashed the party for the fun of it. I was getting bored just standing around listening to all the hullaballoo and decided to leave. I headed over to the bus stop at the corner of Maple and Spring. As I neared the corner, I could see my bus. It paused for a minute then quickly headed down the hill before I could get the driver's attention. Now I would have to wait at least another half-hour for the next one.

I sat on a bench near the bus stop mulling over why I was there in the first place. I didn't seem to fit in this social scene like Larry. Most of the kids that I recognized didn't even acknowledge me. I felt like a total outsider. After several more minutes of self-analysis, I saw a group of kids headed toward the bus stop. They were loud and seemed to be arguing. In the group I saw Larry and a blond with a page boy haircut who was holding hands with one of our classmates, a black kid named Greg. As they got closer, the discussion between Larry and Greg seemed to get even more animated over this girl. I wasn't totally sure what had precipitated this because I had left early.

The next thing I knew Larry was fending off punches from Greg and yelling that he was only kidding about what he said. Several kids broke it up while I just stood by stunned at what I was seeing.

I had never seen Larry in a fight before and had I always thought of him as a pacifist. I was shocked to see this unfold before my eyes. Apparently Larry had said something to Greg that set him off but I don't know what it was. Later Larry whined to me for not helping him when he was getting pummeled by Greg. I don't know what he expected me to do. It was pretty much over by the time I got there and besides, if I did jump in to help, Greg was big enough to kick the snot out of both of us. Besides that, if Larry had said something that was offensive enough to get Greg riled up, I might have been offended too.

Friends should help friends when they're being put upon for no good reason, and I would help in a heartbeat. But if they do something that is wrong and I don't agree with, then I won't. I won't defend the indefensible. But as I said earlier, I really didn't know what set this whole thing off and probably that's a good thing. I guess Larry saw it differently and may still hold that grudge to this day.

CHAPTER THIRTY-FIVE

The Return of Yummy!

I never heard another word from Larry about that incident at the frat party. Soon after, Larry began raving about how convenient and great Callahan's bar was. One night after shooting pool at Whitey's and hitting a few spots downtown, we ended up to Callahan's around midnight. Sitting on the corner of the bar watching a game of nine ball sat a guy named Dan Cauley. He lived on Eighth Street a few blocks north of my house and was one of the regulars Larry knew by his first name. "Hey, Dan, how's it going?" Larry asked.

"Good now, Larry," he replied.

"What do you mean *now?*" asked Larry.

"Well," smirked Dan, "if you were here earlier you'd have seen a quite a battle."

"What kind of battle, a fight?"

"Oh yeah! A real tongue twister of a battle," Dan replied laughing. "One of the funniest things I ever seen until it turned nasty."

"What happened?" I asked Dan, now that he got my interest. I was fascinated hearing about fights but hated being in them because I often ended up on the short side of the stick.

"You guys know Yummy Kiley?" Dan asked.

"Hell yeah," I said. "I've known him since I was a little kid. He moved over this way, didn't he?"

"Yeah, he did," Dan replied. "In fact he's a regular here."

"Oh yeah, I know Yummy too; met him a couple weeks ago," Larry said. "He kicked my ass in a game of eight ball. He's a funny character with that speech impediment of his."

"Boy, you better not say that to him, Larry—he'll kick your ass!"

"I know. He's a pretty tough character," Larry replied.

"Tough ain't the word. I've seen him kick the snot out of guys when he lived on Ferry Street," I said.

"So tell us what happened, Dan." Larry interrupted.

"Ok, ok. Yummy was half in the bag when he came in around ten o'clock with his brother Snowball. I was sitting a couple seats down from this guy I had never seen before. He was drinking Genny Cream Ale like most of us and not saying a word, just watching two guys playing a game of eight ball."

"So get to the point," Larry said impatiently. "We ain't got all night."

"Ok, Ok. I'm getting there. Snowball had bought a round of Gennies for him and Yummy while they were watching the game. Well, Yummy's glass was empty so he turned to Johnny and said, "Give me anudder futting Genny, Johnnie! Give Snowball one too."

"Ok," Johnny replied.

"All of a sudden this stranger says to Johnny, 'give me anudder futtin Genny too,' as he slapped down a couple bucks on the bar."

"What da futt did you juz say?" Yummy yelled to this guy.

"What duh futt's it to ya, azzole?" the guy replied sarcastically.

"You makin fun uh me, you futtin jerk?"

"No, but I still thin yur a futtin azzhole," the guy shot back.

That was it. The next thing you know Yummy was on him like stink on a skunk. He pummeled the crap out of him before Johnny and two other guys could pull Yummy off. Then Snowball and Johnny dragged the guy outside before Yummy could go after him again. I think Yummy broke this guy's nose because it was bleeding like a stuck pig when they got him outta here."

"Calm down, Yummy," Johnny said when he came back in with Snowball.

"I looked out the window and saw the guy holding his nose and staggering across Hoosick Street," Dan said. "Then after Yummy and Snowball left, I asked Johnny who the hell the guy was that Yummy beat up. He said his name was Louie and he'd come in every once in a while. But Johnny always had the toughest time understanding him."

Come to find out this poor guy had the same speech impediment Yummy had. He had been born with a hair lip, and because of it had trouble speaking clearly. He wasn't making fun of Yummy— and Yummy wasn't making fun of him. Neither of them realized they both had the same problem. This guy apparently was harassed at times too. Sadly, this poor schlub didn't realize Yummy was one tough son of a bitch.

CHAPTER THIRTY-SIX

Cents of Worth

So our drinking adventures continued off and on, some together as a group, and some individually. Luckily, we weren't alcoholics. We did what a lot of young people do today—binge drink on weekends. The plus side for us was that we didn't drive; we just drank then either walked home or took the bus. Friday nights were always brimming with shoppers downtown. Many teenagers hung out at Paul's Restaurant, on River Street across from Whitey's pool hall. However, Paul's was mostly a Catholic High hangout. Every Friday night at nine, Paul's held a dance featuring local radio DJ's. The dances were popular among teenagers from all over the city. Paul's wasn't very big inside, so competition for limited spots in the dance hall was pretty intense among kids from the local high schools—Troy, Lansingburg, LaSalle, Watervliet and Catholic High. As you can imagine, these local kids were *parochial* about their turf, which often resulted in brief skirmishes that usually didn't amount to much, because there was always a cop nearby either directing traffic or walking the beat. If the cops saw things getting out of hand, they'd immediately come over and break it up.

The Mayflower Restaurant, located near the Troy Theater just up the street from Paul's, was where many Troy High kids hung out. We affectionately nicknamed the Mayflower, *The Boat.* Clever! Huh? The boat didn't have any live entertainment—just a jukebox. The manager Con Cholakis (who later became a venerable judge) was a fun guy. He loved to tease us when we came in and seemed to know every kid by their first name which is a great skill for a future politician.

Although he loved to joke with the kids, Con didn't tolerate horse play. If you got in trouble with him, you were banned. Since many kids loved to dance, they went out early for burgers at the Boat on Friday nights then meander down to Paul's around 8:30 in hopes of getting into the dance. If they couldn't get in, they'd head back to the boat.

I would normally meet Larry at Whitey's on Friday nights around seven-thirty. Luckily, as I stated earlier, I was able to earn spending money working parttime after school, washing cars at the Hendrick Hudson garage. I didn't earn a lot, but the fact that I was finally able to keep a regular part-time job and earn my own money gave me a sense of pride. It also gave me a glimpse of what it might be like not being poor and not feeling different from my high school buddies.

As high school progressed, I was getting a sense, although muted, that I was being ostracized. Billy and Larry were able to go to the movies or bowling or on a date but I couldn't. They'd grill me about why I didn't join them and I'd come up with some lame excuse. They didn't overtly treat me differently, but I always felt an undercurrent running through my subconscious that I wasn't the same as them. They kind of rolled their eyes and went about having fun without me. I don't think they truly realized how poor our family still was.

The reason I couldn't go most of the time was because I didn't have the money and Ma just didn't have extra money to give to me. Their parents did if they came up short. I know Ma felt bad about it. She realized as a teenager, I'd be missing out on things because I didn't have the money to afford them. But she tried her best to give me a little extra whenever possible. The best part of earning my own money was that I didn't have to burden Ma as much. Earning my own money allowed me to feel like more of an equal, instead of an outsider. Now I could go to a dance, play pool, go bowling and even buy some new clothes. I don't think Billy and Larry ever had to wear hand-me-downs or clothes from the Salvation Army like I did, or maybe they did and never told me. Of course, Larry didn't have hand-me-downs; he was an only child.

To their credit, Larry and Billy's parents did instill a strong work ethic in them and insisted they get part-time jobs. Billy worked as a bus boy at Woolworth's, while Larry got a job selling shoes parttime at Endicott Johnson's. Although their parents were middle class, raising teenagers was still a demanding and expensive proposition. The advantage that Billy and Larry had over me was that they at least had two parents to guide them most of the time, although they both lost their fathers while they were teenagers.

Larry was an only child. His dad was a World War II veteran and a real nice guy with a fun personality, and his mom was open and friendly, albeit a bit more reserved. Larry said his dad was a great dart player, which I can believe, because Larry was pretty decent at darts too. Sadly, Larry's dad was a heavy smoker, a habit that led to his untimely death from lung cancer.

On the other hand, Billy's family seemed slightly dysfunctional like mine. However, unlike mine, both his parents worked. Billy's mom was a nurse; his father was a laborer and several years older. Additionally, they liked having a few brews at the end of a hard day, which may be the reason they bickered almost as much as my parents did. Billy's relationship with his dad was the antithesis of my brother Cliff's relationship to my dad. Billy and his dad always seemed totally intolerant of each other and argued constantly when I was there. On the other hand, although my brother Cliff was usually the target of my dad's abuse, he rarely argued with him. Instead, he just laughed it off most of the time.

Sadly, my friendship with Billy and Larry has diminished over time. We're still friends but rarely see or speak to each other. However, we still exchange Christmas cards every year. In retrospect, I wonder if Billy and Larry really accepted me as we got older. They may have thought they did, but I felt at times that they didn't. Why, I asked myself. Was it because I was from a poor family? I don't know. Maybe it was just my imagination—I sure hope so. The one thing I'm sure of—I did get that feeling at times.

On the other hand, I never felt that way about Ronnie. I never sensed he didn't accept me. He never looked down his nose at me. Ronnie always seemed upbeat in school—with an easy smile, a ready joke, and rarely appeared angry. He lived on Fifteenth Street with his mom, a housewife, dad, an insurance salesman, two brothers and an eccentric older sister. Even though we were friends, I wasn't as close to Ronnie as I was to Billy and Larry during my school years. Ironically, Ronnie and I have remained close friends into our adult lives.

CHAPTER THIRTY-SEVEN

Why Did He Go?

Billy started dating Rose later in his junior year as well as working more hours. So I hung out more with Larry since he didn't have a steady girlfriend yet. If Larry was working late at EJ's (Endicott Johnson's Shoe Store), he would usually arrive at Whitey's around nine. Normally, when I got there early I practiced or hung out and bullshitted with Bugsy Mumfry, a local pool hustler and a regular at Whitey's. When Larry finally arrived, he'd usually brag about all the panties he'd seen that day while peaking up ladies' dresses as helped them try on new shoes. He even described how many of them didn't wear panties and how he'd seen their *bearded clams*. Of course I didn't believe it.

Occasionally, if he wasn't working at Woolworth's or out with Rose, Billy and I stopped by EJ's to bust on Larry about his outrageous claims. Being our buddy and knowing we were young letches too, Larry strategically positioned mirrors on the floor so that we could get a peak of his customers' panties too. Better still, their *bearded clams*. Unfortunately, I never got to see a bearded clam there. But, being young and eternally horny, we were grateful to see anything close to a woman's sexuality. Larry was destined to be a good salesman later in life because he was such a smooth, clever talker. He could out bullshit a bull shitter, he was that good.

When Larry finally arrived at Whitey's, we'd shoot a little pool then head out in our unending crusade to lose our virginity either with some unwitting maiden or some old hag at one of the local watering holes—Duke's, Dempsey's or the Siena Club. Although this was our weekly ritual, we somehow always managed to keep our virginity intact, no matter how adroit Larry's line of BS. The only thing we were successful in doing each week was getting shit faced, staggering home, and continuing our quest in the privacy of our minds and bedrooms.

I was very upset that warm Saturday morning when I arrived at Whitey's pool hall. Larry had stiffed me again the previous night. We were supposed to go drinking at Duke's and continue our futile journey toward manhood. I had just turned eighteen—the legal drinking age—in January of that year and always ended up getting drinks for Larry wherever we went. He was still underage and I think that was one of the reasons he hung out with me so much. I had arrived at Whitey's around eight, the time we were supposed to meet, shoot some pool and head out on our quest. However, Larry never showed up. I waited about an hour before I went over to Bugsy Mumfry and asked if he'd seen Larry.

"Oh yea, he was here around 7:30 with Tommy Beresny. But they left just before you got here."

"Did he say where they were going?"

"He mentioned something about going to the Villa Valente with Tommy's brother John."

"Shit! I can't believe he left without me again, the dick-head. He knew I was going to be here at eight. They could have waited for me."

"Well, Hydie, I don't know what to tell you."

"Don't call me Hydie!" I angrily shouted back. "I hate that." Bugsy knew I was pissed and didn't say another word. I played a rack by myself then decided to head up to the Bowlatorium on River and Hoosick Streets in hopes that Billy or his brother Art might be there. They liked to bowl a lot and often hung out there when Billy wasn't working.

Tired from the long five block trek, I could barely open the heavy glass door that led into the bowling area. As luck would have it, I discovered they weren't there. Now more depressed than angry, I went into the bar. After one beer I decided to head to the Troy Bowl in hopes Billy and Art might be there. Plus, if they weren't there, I only had to go a couple more blocks to my house. The Troy Bowl was new, having opened the previous summer, and sported a nice bar and served sandwiches as well as booze. If I was lucky, Mary, an effervescent, well-endowed red head might be working. The eight block walk calmed my anger over getting stiffed by Larry.

The Troy Bowl was on Sixth Avenue near the RPI approach, and as I got closer my hopes began to rise. I anticipated that Bill and Art had decided to bowl there instead of the Bowlatorium. However, when I opened the door and surveyed the twenty-five lanes of league bowlers, I soon realized they weren't there. "Damn it!" I quietly cursed to myself as my anger returned. "What a shitty night this is turning out to be." Lonely, depressed and without that pretty barmaid to ease my pain, I spent the next couple hours whining in my Fitzie's beer, all the while stuffing my face full of crackers loaded with Kaukauna Klub cheese. I was soon shit faced and staggered up the hill to my house around midnight. I walked in without saying a word, fell into bed and faded into alcohol- clouded sleep.

Slightly hung over and still steaming about the night before, I was in no mood for company as I was shooting pool by myself at Whitey's the next morning. Usually, I never stayed angry very long. But this time was an exception. I just couldn't seem to shake my mood. That was when this kid I had seen around school but didn't really know approached me. "Hi! Do you want to shoot some eight ball?"

Still in a vile mood, I looked up, shook my head and said, "Nah. I'm not in much of a mood to play today." The disappointment in his eyes would become ensconced in my memory.

"Ok. Sorry to bother you." There was an ominous tone of sadness and disappointment in his voice. But even that didn't change my mind or my mood. With his head down, he silently walked back to his seat a couple of tables away. A few minutes later I watched him head down the stairs and I felt a chill come over my soul. I tried to shake it, but it lingered with me the rest of the day. Normally, I would have loved to have someone ask me to play because they rarely did. I wasn't that good and most of the players who hung out there knew that. Usually, I just played with Larry, Billy, Tom, my brother-in-law Andy and on rare occasions, Bugsy.

About an hour later I decided to go the movies at the Troy Theater. I always felt comforted in the cool darkness of this classic theater and could escape my real world troubles. My mind could retreat from the anger and angst I was experiencing from being disrespected and disregarded. It was in the seclusion of this regal theater that I was able to regain some balance and equilibrium and slowly release my pent-up anger through the medium of art and fantasy that movies provided me. (To this day I still go to the movies and find solace and relief from whatever emotional stress I may be under.)

Larry finally called late Saturday afternoon when I got home from the movies and offered a lame excuse about why he had stiffed me the night before. I didn't buy it and didn't really care at that point, having purged my anger in the movies earlier. He then asked me if I wanted to go bowling with Billy, Art, and him at the Troy Bowl that night. It was open bowling so we could easily get a lane and hopefully flirt with Mary the barmaid after bowling. It was fun bowling that night even though Art cleaned our clocks, bowling a couple 200 plus games, while we struggled to break 100. However, the highlight of the evening was watching the cleavage between Mary's knockers as she bent over the beer cooler. By midnight we were all slurring our words and waving to a smiling, mischievous Mary, who loved playing along with our testosterone-driven banter. We headed out the door drunk with our virginity still intact. The quest would have to continue another day.

I awoke Sunday morning to the smell of bacon sizzling in Ma's cast iron skillet. My head didn't feel too bad for a change after what I put it through the night before. However, that would shortly change as I listened to the local news on our rickety, static-filled radio. In a somber tone the announcer sadly declared, "Tragedy struck yesterday afternoon at a local swimming hole on the Poestenkill Creek." I knew that swimming-hole. I had been there many several times in years past. My heart stood still. "Oh my God," I thought as a cold chill ran down my spine, similar to the one I felt the day before at Whitey's. "No, it couldn't be him. Could it?"

The radio announcer continued, "Philip Aston, a seventeen year old junior at Troy High drowned after diving into the swirling rapids of a swimming hole the locals called 95. He apparently hit his head on a submerged rock and never returned to the surface. His body was retrieved by members of the Troy Fire Department rescue squad, who were called to the scene by other swimmers who witnessed the accident."

"Oh my God," I screamed to Ma as I burst into tears. "I know that kid."

Stunned by my outburst of grief, Ma rushed over to console me. "Herbie, are you ok? How do you know him? You never mentioned him before."

"I only knew him from school, Ma. He wasn't a friend." Soon, guilt and grief consumed me as I explained to Ma exactly what transpired that day at Whitey's. "If only I had played pool with him, he'd be alive right now. It's my fault," I cried.

"Herbie, it's not your fault. It's God's will," Ma soothed, holding me tight, trying her best to console me. "He probably would have gone swimming that day anyway, even if you had played pool with him. You can't blame yourself."

"But, I can't help it, Ma. I knew something bad was going to happen when I saw him. Something didn't seem right. Maybe it wouldn't have happened if I'd played."

"Herbie," Ma said softly, "what you experienced was a premonition, a signal of something that might happen in the future. Many people experience them. They're beyond your control. It's not your fault. It was his fate in life. God chooses when to take us and He decided it was this boy's time."

It took me a long time to quietly get over the guilt I felt after his death. But with time, I was able to come to the realization that Ma was right. It wasn't my fault. It was this kid's fate and that wouldn't have changed no matter what I did that day. However, I also believe that God had given me a life's lesson about how we should not let our negative emotions dictate how we treat people. This boy was an innocent bystander who tried to befriend me. But, because I was still upset about the night before, I let my negative emotions prevent me from possibly making a new friend. I know if the tables were turned, I would have felt hurt and rejected too. God knows how many times I had experienced that rejection and pain in my young life.

Boy, Did I Get Fried!

On occasion I hung out at the bars with my buddies. Looking back now, I can see how some guys who were what I called secondary level friends can manipulate you and your closest friends to the detriment of your overall relationships. I found that to be true with Tommy Beresny. He wasn't an overtly evil guy, but he was a manipulator. I think he might have been the wedge that came between me and Larry on occasion. One example was when we all went out to hit a few bars downtown. Tommy didn't have much money with him, or so he said. Because of that, Larry and I paid his way most of the night with the promise that he would make it up to us at another time. Right!

Larry decided to go home early that night because he had to be at EJ's at nine the next morning. Since I didn't have to be at the garage until Saturday afternoon, I figured I'd tag along with Tommy. He wanted to go to Gages Bar and Grill in the Burgh to shoot some pool or maybe pick up some chicks. That idea about the chicks definitely perked up my interest. So we hopped on the Fifth Ave bus and got to Gage's around ten o'clock.

The place was kind of empty except for a couple of vagrants sitting in the corner and two couples sitting at the far end of the bar kibitzing with Jen the barmaid. After shooting a couple games of darts and a game of eight ball, I told Tommy I was going home and get a good night's sleep for a change. However, Tommy insisted we walk a few blocks north to Ted's Fish Fry because he was starved and a fish fry was cheap. So being the sucker I am, I agreed to go with him. When we got to Ted's, Tommy rifled through his pockets then turned to me and said, "Shit, I'm out of money. I only have enough left for bus fare home. Can you pay for mine? I'll pay you the next week."

Although I was leery, I was hungry myself and told him I'd buy him a fish fry and Coke. I then asked him to order one for me, heavy on the sauce and a vanilla shake because I had to go to the john. "Yeah sure," he said as I handed him my last five dollar bill and headed to the men's room. When I got back, he was sitting in a booth with four fish orders, some French fries, onion rings and a Coke lined up in front of him. Opposite him sat my fish fry and shake, which looked half full. "Here's your change," he said, handing me a dollar bill and two quarters.

I was pissed! "You told me you only wanted a fish fry and a Coke. How come you bought all this other crap?" I said angrily. Then I looked up at the menu, saw the prices and realized that on top of buying all this extra food, he was stiffing me out of fifty cents. "What a lousy dickhead!" I thought to myself. "Jesus, Tommy, cough up the extra fifty cents you owe me right now!"

"Oh yea, I forgot I had two extra quarters in my pocket. Here you go," he said, as he launched into his second fish fry. Boy, did I regret going out with him. It was the first time I had done this without Larry or Billy and swore to myself that I wouldn't be suckered by him again. When I think back now, he reminded me of a guy in the Popeye cartoons named J. Wellington Wimpy, generally referred simply to as Wimpy. He was the perfect role model for Tommy: lazy, cowardly, a glutten, and a scam artist of the highest order. Wimpy's best known phrase was, "I'll gladly pay you on Tuesday for a hamburger today." In Tommy's case it became: "Can you pay for mine? I'll pay you next week." The truth is he never paid me, period!

CHAPTER THIRTY-NINE

Broadening My Interests?

I entered my senior year with high expectations for myself, especially in art, where I continued to excel. I hoped I could find a way to go to college after high school and become an art teacher and coach. Although I struggled with my grades early on in high school, I was eventually able to improve them as well as my standardized test scores. After reviewing my records and noticing steady improvement, my guidance counselor Mr. Murray felt I had a bright future ahead. He suggested a couple of schools and highly recommended Farmingdale State College on Long Island because it had a great art program. His confidence made me feel very upbeat as I began my senior year.

In addition, I had started doing things I hadn't done previously. I had become a fire monitor under Mr. Henry's guidance during my junior year. He was now my art teacher and persuaded me to do some work for the sectional basketball games that were held each year at our gym. I would hand paint signs that would be hung in the gym rafters during sectional play. I actually became pretty good at sign painting because of it.

Sadly, as I mentioned earlier, I gave up on competitive sports after being unceremoniously cut from the varsity basketball team by Coach Kurse or Coach Howland or both because I had a fight with Steve Dawalski. The fact that they decided to go against precedent and not allow me to play junior varsity after I was cut from varsity made it an easy decision for me. I decided it wasn't worth the aggravation anymore. I lost the fire in my belly needed to continue after I realized they weren't going to allow me to play at any level. In doing so I had unknowingly gained a small sense of maturity in my young life about the importance or non-importance people place on sports. However, I did enjoy playing intramural basketball and pick-up games at various city parks during the coming years. I found those games satisfied my urge to compete. I didn't need to be a varsity athlete to have fun. Sports should be fun. I guess you could say my junior year was a seminal year of transition and change for me. It's odd how certain moments and events in a person's life can do that. I found that I had more fun playing drums during the basketball games than I had sitting on the bench as a player during the games. During that year the band also started playing at the RPI field house for our varsity hockey games. It was a thrill being on that iconic bandstand that was home to RPI's pep band. Viewing the games from the stage also gave me a different perspective of how the game was played— a unique vantage point where I could see and hear the hitting, passing and shooting up close.

I also became more involved in chorus as well as the drama club. I was lucky enough to get a small role in our first play. It was a story about an Irish potato farmer, named Seamus Mcguirk, his wife Chloe, and their struggle to survive during the Great Potato Famine of the 1845. During the weeks leading up to opening night, I made a new set of friends. One girl in particular, Cheryl Nizmore, made a lasting impression on me. She played the lead role as Seamus' wife. Seamus was a salty character but she was even saltier. Cheryl was really talented and pretty too, with her Irish brogue resonating across the stage when yelling at poor Seamus. "Arrgh, Seamus, yer wits ave gone astray, they ave!" She yelled at poor Seamsus as he sat at the kitchen table downing a Guinness and smoking his pipe.

After a terrific opening night performance her parents invited the entire cast to their house on Saturday night for a party celebrating the successful inaugural year of the drama club. Her father was a professor at RPI and her mother was a stay-at-home mom. They lived on the Troy Country Club Road in a leased brick, ranch style home with a beautiful landscaped yard, white picket fence and circular driveway. It looked like a mansion to me and nothing like the wood framed three family apartment house where I lived.

Because I didn't have a means of getting to her house, Cheryl arranged to have her dad pick me up at my house. I was very apprehensive about him doing that but I really wanted to go. I had a sense that he might look down his nose at me because of where I lived, being a professor and all. I guess I had an underlying sense of being from a different social class than them. However, he proved me wrong. He was so nice and friendly when he picked me up. "Hi, Herbie, I've heard a lot of good things about you."

Wow, I was shocked to hear that. "Thank you, Mr. Nizmore," I replied.

"How long have you lived here, Herbie?"

"We moved here when I was one, but I was born in Swanton, Vermont."

"So you're a native Catamount!" he laughed.

Not knowing the nickname of the University of Vermont, I just agreed. "I...guess so," I replied.

We then headed off in his Chevy Brookwood station wagon. He told me when he first came to RPI he used to walk by my house quite often. He really loved the old architecture in some of the houses, especially the row houses where I lived. (It's funny how some people looked at them as dumps and he looked at them as gems...go figure.) He told me how he taught an architecture class about the history of American cities, and that Troy's architecture was magnificent. He raved about the Troy Music Hall, the public library, the churches, the Tiffany windows and the brownstones dotting the city. By the time I arrived at their house, I was much more at ease and better informed. I learned more about the architecture of our city in twenty minutes than I did in my entire life.

We were greeted in the driveway by Cheryl. "Hi, Herbie," she said. "Come on! I'll show you the neighborhood."

"Ok", I replied.

"Your Dad's a nice guy Cheryl," I told her, as we headed toward the golf course.

"I'm lucky," she said. "Both my parents are great."

I thought to myself how lucky she really was. My Mom was great and tried to do what was best for us kids with the limited help and resources she had. I still loved my Dad and wanted to think he was great too, but then I remembered how he left us and how he was not around most of my early life—a time I really could have used a Dad. I missed the kind of connection she had with her dad. As we walked along, she told me how he took her for walks, planned camping outings, taught her to swim and encouraged her to pursue her dreams.

I didn't have a romantic interest in Cheryl, even though she was very pretty; I just liked the fact we had things in common to talk about. We both loved being in being in this play. Plus we also had several other interests: tennis, swimming, music and art. But as our walk came to an end, she suddenly became quiet as we approached her house. "Are you ok?" I asked, sensing something was bothering her.

"Uh...not really...just...we're moving after school lets out."

My heart sank for a minute. My mind began racing back to grade school when I lost Lois to a job transfer and never saw her again. However, this time I didn't have a romantic connection...yet. "I'm sorry to hear that, Cheryl. Where are you moving to?"

"California. Dad got a full professorship at Cal Poly," She whispered. "It's a huge career move for our family. But I'm so sad. I will miss all my friends here."

"But you'll make plenty of new ones," I tried to assure her.

"I know...I know. But it's so hard," she said with tears welling up in the corner of her eyes. "This is the third time in six years that we have moved."

My heart was aching for her but I didn't know how to comfort her other than to tell her that how bad I felt for her. Just as I was about to hug her, a car pulled in her drive way and out popped several cast members laughing and waving at us. Seeing them, she immediately brightened up and whispered to me: "Thank you, Herbie, you're a nice guy....I'll be all right."

She then greeted the others and we all walked into the house together. Soon the other guests arrived and within a few minutes their dining room and parlor were filled with guests. They were neighbors and colleagues from RPI. Her mom had set up an elaborate buffet table with chafing dishes containing Swedish meatballs, chicken and a pasta dish. In a large glass bowl were dozens of giant, chilled shrimp and a separate glass bowl with cocktail sauce. Lemon slices circled the bowl of shrimp. I had never eaten shrimp although I had seen them in the Fulton Fish Market on Congress Street as a kid and at Sonny's wedding. I always wondered what they tasted like and now I would have a chance to find out.

"Herbie, you got to try one of these," Dave, one of the cast members, said, as he bit into one.

I was a little leery at first but decided to take the plunge. It tasted a bit strange at first, but after double dipping it in cocktail sauce I began to acquire a taste for them. Within seconds, I had a pile of shrimp skeletons on my crystal plate. Within twenty minutes or so, I had feasted on a dozen Swedish meatballs and God only knows how many shrimp, pasta salad and lemon delight for dessert I consumed. I was stuffed.

Most of the guests seemed nice as they walked up to us and told us how great the show was, while others huddled in small enclaves, holding their half-filled wine glasses and cocktail napkins as they discussed the politics of the day. As coffee was offered, a middle aged, dark-haired lady in a flowered print dress with a silk scarf wrapped around her bejeweled neck called for a toast to the cast.

"Here, here!" everyone replied in unison. That's when she asked that the cast reprise her favorite scene from the play. Luckily, all the cast members in that particular act had come to the party. Although we were caught off guard by her request, we still performed the act perfectly to the delight of everyone. It was really interesting for me to meet this kind of people. Some were a bit snooty but most were down to earth and sincere.

When Cheryl's Dad took me home around nine o'clock, I thanked him then waved as I headed up the porch where Ma and my sister Patty were sitting on this extremely warm night. How did it go, Herbie?" Ma asked.

"It was fun, but I was a little nervous in the beginning," I replied.

"What did you have to eat?" Patty asked sarcastically. "Did they have a fu fu platter?"

"What's the heck's a fu fu platter?" I asked sincerely.

"She's teasing you, Herbie," Ma said, turning to Patty. "Stop being snotty to him."

"Well, he thinks he's hot stuff since he got in the drama club."

"No, I don't!" I replied honestly.

Ma then said, "Stop the nonsense, both of you." I described the lavish menue: Swedish meatballs, chicken rosemary and lots and lots of shrimp. Ma was quite impressed with that and Patty just said, "yuk" and stomped off into the house.

"What did I do to her that she's in such a rotten mood?" I asked Ma after Patty left.

"Nothing, Herbie, She's just angry because Andy wouldn't take her to the drive-in tonight, that's all. She'll get over it."

With that we both headed back into the house for the night. Lying in bed, I started thinking about everything that happened that day, as well as everything that happened during high school.

Most of the people I met that evening were in a different world from me and my family. Many were nice but I remember sensing that some acted superior, like they were better than me. The Nizmores weren't like many of the other folks there. They were down to earth and unpretentious. I really liked them. I was beginning to realize that even in America everything wasn't equal. It may be known as the land of opportunity, but not necessarily the land of equal opportunity.

CHAPTER FORTY

Oh, Henry!

One of our teachers, Mr. Henry was an iconic character: he was completely bald, often nicknamed Mr. Cue-ball, usually attired in black, and when he wore his fedora, it was always askew. He was well known in the city for being the unofficial fire chief because he ended up going to just about every major fire in the city. In fact, he had a special fire alarm in his classroom. When it rang for the first time, he was all ears. But if it rang for a second alarm, he would be off to the races. How he was allowed to leave school like he did still amazes me. Some firefighters may have considered him a gadfly because of his critique of what was going on at a particular fire. But others respected his vast knowledge about firefighting. In fact, later in life he was honored by the Troy Fire Department for his volunteer work promoting fire safety in the school system and across the community at large.

To his credit Mr. Henry tried to help me get a part time job doing silk screening at the Peerless Company on River Street. However, I procrastinated applying for the job and Jimmy Halse's brother Bruce got the job instead of me. I really regret not getting that job because it would have motivated me even further to continue my dream of being an artist and teacher.

To make matters even worse, I discovered Bruce was dating a pretty blond girl I had met at Beman Park one brilliant, fall afternoon. After playing ball for a couple hours at Beman Park, I was bushed. But instead of heading home that Saturday, I started daydreaming while sitting on the top of the hill overlooking Tibbett's

Avenue. I was deep in thought when out of the corner of my eye I saw this angelic beauty approaching me. I was shocked when she asked if she could sit with me. "Sure," I said, totally surprised. "Hi, what's your name?" I asked sheepishly.

"Sherry," she replied.

"My name's Herb."

"I know," she said.

"You do?" I asked, intrigued that she knew my name. I was stunned. I couldn't remember ever seeing her before but I was amazed how easily she was able to spark a conversation. We talked about things we did downtown, how she liked to dance as I did, and everything under the sun. So as usually happens with me and girls, I was quickly becoming enamored of her. That damned stupid Cupid was shooting darts at my heart again. I wish he'd miss once in a while because just as I was about to ask for her phone number, Bruce came ambling up the hill and gruffly told her they had to get going. She got up, smiled at me and said goodbye.

"It was nice talking to you, Sherry," I said, as she glided away with a smile and a nod. After they left, I began the torturous process of removing those darts from my heart as all the emotions I experienced earlier bled out of me.

CHAPTER FORTY-ONE

For the Good Times

And so time kept marching on, and as it marched, things began to change for me. I felt a growing undercurrent of panic because things were changing so fast. Although change is inevitable, it's not always easy. I was finding out first hand that change is the only real constant in life, and learning to deal with it would be a huge challenge.

In the meantime, my buddies and classmates were determined to make our senior year a memorable one—one that none of us would soon forget, including our teachers and administration. Many of us turned eighteen that year and could now drink legally. We spent many a Friday or Saturday night in South Troy at the Snuggery Inn or at Ma Foley's in West Sand Lake. Ma Foley's soon became the favorite watering hole for our class where we'd go to drink and dance on Saturday nights. Foley's house band, Jack Welsh and the Melodeons, played there every Saturday night for decades. You couldn't beat it. The beer was cheap and the entertainment was free.

Each weekend we looked forward to seeing the same older couples who had been going there for years. They wore the same outfits week after week. The men usually wore colorful jackets and ties, while their wives wore poufy white blouses. A few even wore a blinking red light inside their blouse. Maybe they used to work in the red light district at Mame Faye's brothel when they were younger—who, knows! They certainly were fun, classy characters, who livened up the place and always seemed to have a great time.

On the first of January, 1962, my final few months of school engulfed me, and a challenging new era surreptitiously began to creep into our national psyche. The Vietnam war would cynically change the way our country viewed war forever. The expression "Where were you in 62'?" seems quite poignant to me now. That year was a transformational period for both me and our country as the Vietnam War loomed menacingly on the horizon.

In addition, my neighborhood had inexorably changed. Evisceration of my neighborhood started to accelerate at an alarming rate with only a few neighbors remaining. Home after home and business after business was ripped down. Ferry Street and Congress Street evaporated into the fog of history. Much of Eighth Street and College Avenue soon followed suit. Our tiny, moribund enclave lasted just a few more years, but its legacy and humanity will live forever.

Ironically, it was shortly after my high school graduation that I would find out my Dad had gotten a job with the city a couple years earlier. He was now driving a truck for the water department. He had gotten the job through his old drinking buddy, John Buckley, who eventually became Troy City Manager for more than a decade. Of course, Dad didn't help out Ma financially as far as I know. How cruel it seems that our family suffered and struggled all those years, and now my father ends up with a good job after most of his kids had grown up and moved out on their own.

CHAPTER FORTY-TWO

And Now the End Draws Near

As graduation day approached, our class became more and more daring. Several girls ended up pregnant and one of our class favorites, Hank Marcy, was not allowed to attend graduation because he got caught drag racing in front of school the week before. Hank, who looked a lot like James Dean, was a great mechanic and had won the National Automobile Trouble Shooting competition that year—a great honor for our auto mechanics class as well as our school.

Our senior class picnic lowered the standard for all other classes to follow. It was held at Lake George, where senior classes had been having their picnics for years. We arrived in yellow school buses at the Million Dollar Beach before boarding the Mini-Ha-Ha for a two hour cruise. (Sort of like Gilligan's Island, without Gilligan or the Island.) Several kids were half loaded by the time we got there. Others would soon follow.

Karla, a cheerleader known mostly for her big boobs, sat on the beach in her bathing suit guzzling screw drivers. At the same time, her friends tried unsuccessfully to throw our class chaperone Ms. Mercer into the chilly lake against her will. Then crazy Tom Beresny unscrewed several water fountain nozzles, making the beach look like Yellowstone National Park when Old Faithful erupted. This all happened before we even boarded the boat.

Once onboard, things settled down a bit. I ended up playing poker and won eleven bucks. I only had a couple beers because I didn't want to get drunk and spoil my day. But other kids couldn't stop chugging them down. Coming back to shore, a couple kids got into a scuffle over something stupid and one of them threw a beer bottle through a plate glass window, scattering shards of glass everywhere. That little tirade cost our class forty dollars to repair the damage. Unbelievably, no one got arrested or seriously hurt that day.

Because of our class stupidity and egregious behavior, the following year my sister Brenda's Senior Class had to plead to be allowed to go to Lake George for their picnic. Why our class got so out of control that year is beyond me. Ironically, some of the kids who did these stupid things were supposedly the social elite of our class. As it turns out, they really were *Bucksters.*

The night before our final graduation rehearsal, a bunch of us kids went to Ma Foley's to celebrate. I stayed for a little while then hitched a ride home with Ronnie because I was tired and bored. Ronnie was our designated driver back then because he didn't drink. When I got to school the next morning, several of those same kids who had gone to Ma Foley's the night before, were asleep on the steps leading up to the gym. They had stayed out all night and were still half loaded at nine o'clock in the morning.

My senior year had been full with all the good, bad and sad times but in the end, it flew by. I loved my high school experience and never missed a day of school during my four years. With graduation at hand, I was beginning to feel an undercurrent of grieving. Graduation day should have been a happy time for me, a milestone for what I had accomplished during those four wonderful years. Instead it was a day twinged with melancholy. I knew things would never be the same for me. I was entering a new, uncharted period of my life.

I remembered back in biology class during my sophomore year when skinny Ms. Green prodded me to continue studying the sciences. For some reason, she thought I was smarter than I thought I was and that I could do really well if I applied myself. I had an A average all year long but only got a 90 on my Regents exam and she seemed disappointed that I didn't ace it. Today I think a 90 was pretty good for me. On the flip side, I remember how Mrs. Mercer hounded me for being such a lousy typist during my junior year. She didn't let up with that or my business math class where I scrounged a C average most of the year but ended up with a B in my final non-Regents exam. However, the thing that took the cake was my final non-Regents typing exam. I made no typing mistakes at all and typed 35 words per minute—ten better than I averaged all year. I figured I nailed it and got 100! But there was one slight problem: I had typed the envelope upside down. As punishment, she gleefully gave me a 90 instead of 100. Can you believe that: no typing mistakes, 35 words per minute, envelope typed perfectly, except upside down and she deducts 10 points? To me that's cruel and unusual punishment.

CHAPTER FORTY-THREE

And So It Ends

Although I didn't go to the junior prom (considered the pinnacle of social events during our four years in high school), I did go to our senior dance. In fact I went to the dance with Eileen Gibby, Sue's pretty cousin. Kind of funny how Sue didn't have an interest in me and Eileen apparently did. I think back now that maybe Eileen actually liked me and I never knew it. Hopefully it wasn't a sympathy date contrived by one of my friends to make me feel good. But even if it was, I had a great time.

Some kids went off to college like I wanted to do but couldn't. I wanted to be an art teacher and coach, remember. Others soon went off to fight in service to their country during the Vietnam War. Some never returned, having made the ultimate sacrifice. Others who didn't go to college or into the service got jobs, married and raised a family here in Troy, while some moved away to start a new life elsewhere.

On graduation day, a bright sunny morning, families took pictures to memorialize the event. Some held graduation parties that afternoon, evening or maybe that weekend. But my family didn't. I still had heaviness in my heart and didn't want one. My sister Dorothy would have gone out of her way to have a party for me, but I was insistent. Instead, she attended the ceremony along with Patty and Brenda. She gave me a nice card with some money as did other members of my family. They weren't rich, but they no longer considered themselves poor. Now most of my older siblings had jobs and families of their own to attend to.

I remember standing outside the gym in my cap and gown as Dorothy snapped pictures of me and a couple more with Billy, Larry and Ronnie. Of course we had to whack each other in the nuts once more for old time's sake when no one was looking before we headed our separate ways. Larry's mom was there and Billy's sister who lived in Rensselaer even came with her daughter to celebrate the occasion. I knew Ma couldn't sit through the almost three-hour ceremony but was proud of me and had a beautiful cake waiting when I got home to honor my special day. Most of my of my class- mates were smiling and congratulating each other for making it through and talking about whose party they were going to. Just as we were about to go home, Jimmy Minano, who was in my history class, came over and invited me to his house for a party later that afternoon. He said lots of kids would be there.

"You should go, Herbie, It will be good for you" Dorothy said. One plus, he lived a block west of Dorothy's house on Adams Street so it would be easy to get there. In fact, Dorothy said she would drop me off and pick me up if I wanted to go. I shook his hand and thanked him and told him I would think about it.

"I hope you come," he said as his sister Bernice grabbed him so they could have their picture taken together. I think they were the only family graduating siblings that year. As they were leaving, I thanked him again and told him I would try to make if I could.

When we got home, Ma had a small feast laid out for us includ- ing: cold cuts for sandwiches, salads, fresh fruit, chips and dips and a huge cake covered with creamy vanilla frosting and the words "Troy High's Best graduate: Herbie" piped in purple and gold let- tering. Ma gave me a big hug and told me how proud she was of me. Even with all the heartfelt congratulations from my brothers and sisters and a few remaining neighbors who stopped by, a sense of melancholy still lingered beneath my half-hearted smile.

Around 2:30 most of the people had begun to filter out of the house, and I just sat there for a while silently reading my graduation cards and thinking, "Is this all there is? What am I going to do with myself when college starts in the fall and I don't go?" It was at that moment I knew I had to get out of the house for a while. I had to cheer up so I decided to go to Jimmy's party.

I drove with Dorothy down to her house then walked the half block to the party. In the back of my mind I figured going to this party would cheer me up. But it didn't. Instead it made me even more depressed as I watched the in-crowd kids I didn't really know or associate with laugh and joke with each other. I sat quietly in the corner sucking on a Genny Cream Ale, taking it all in as they made fools of themselves. They were playing a dumb game they called giggle belly. In this game, kids lay down in the middle of the floor with their heads on another person's belly and started laughing hysterically as their bellies heaved up and down along with the girls' skirts. The only interesting part of the whole game was that I saw Sue Melnick's panties. I didn't get it and decided to go back to Dorothy's so she could take me home. After thanking Jimmy and his mom for inviting me, I left, but not feeling quite as bad as when I came. That silly game made me realize that what lies ahead couldn't be as bad as that stupid game. I knew my status in life and was happy having a good family and good friends I would treasure my entire life. I never needed or wanted to be part of the in-crowd and was glad that I never had been part of it.